Did You Spot the Gorilla?

Professor Richard Wiseman began his working life as an award-winning professional magician and was one of the youngest members of The Magic Circle. He obtained a first class honours degree in Psychology from University College London, a doctorate in psychology from Edinburgh University, and was awarded the prestigious Perrott-Warrick Scholarship from Trinity College Cambridge. He now heads a research unit based within the Psychology Department at the University of Hertfordshire.

Professor Wiseman's research has been widely reported in many of the world's leading science journals, and he has presented his findings at numerous national and international academic conferences.

He has featured on hundreds of radio and television programmes, and feature articles about his work have appeared in *The Times*, the *Daily Telegraph* and the *Guardian*. He has also devised several large-scale experiments involving thousands of people. Many of these have been carried out in collaboration with the *Daily Telegraph* and the BBC science programme *Tomorrow's World*.

Also by Richard Wiseman

The Luck Factor

Did You Spot the Gorilla?

How to Recognise Hidden Opportunities

Richard Wiseman

arrow books

Published in Arrow Books in 2004

1 3 5 7 9 10 8 6 4 2

Arrow Books
The Random House Group Limited
20 Vauxhall Bridge Road, London SW1V 2SA

Random House Australia (Pty) Limited
20 Alfred Street, Milsons Point, Sydney,
New South Wales 2061, Australia

Random House New Zealand Limited,
18 Poland Road, Glenfield,
Auckland 10, New Zealand

Random House (Pty) Limited
Endulini, 5A Jubilee Road, Parktown 2193, South Africa

Random House Group Limited Reg. No. 954009
www.randomhouse.co.uk

A CIP catalogue record for this book is available from the British Library

Papers used by Random House
are natural, recyclable products made from wood grown in
sustainable forests. The manufacturing processes conform to
the environmental regulations of the country of origin

ISBN 0 09 946643 0

Typeset by SX Composing DTP, Rayleigh, Essex
Printed and bound in Great Britain by
Bookmarque Ltd, Croydon, Surrey

To Caroline

Acknowledgements

This book would not have been possible without the wonderful guidance of my agent Patrick Walsh, and editors, Anna Cherrett, Lindsay Davies, and Nikola Scott. I am also grateful to the University of Hertfordshire for supporting this work, Emma Greening for helping with the research and to Professor Dan Simons for producing the original 'gorilla' footage. Finally, very special thanks to Caroline Watt for providing assistance at every stage of the process, including invaluable grammatical corrections and sharp-eyed proof checking. Without you Caroline, this book simply would never have happened in its present form, for years to come.

Illustrations by DOW.

Contents

INTRODUCTION
Monkey Business

The hardest thing to do is see what is right in front
of your eyes.
Johann Wolfgang von Goethe, German poet and novelist

Master magician Harry Houdini once amazed the world by making an elephant completely vanish. You are going to perform a version of this incredible illusion, right here, right now.

Take a look at the illustration on page 2. On the left is Houdini and on the right is an elephant. As you can clearly see, the elephant is in full view, and there are no suspicious-looking trap doors or mirrors.

Close your left eye, hold the book at arm's length and look at Houdini's head with your right eye. Now slowly bring the book towards your face, but make sure that you keep looking at Houdini's head with your right eye. At some point, usually when the book is about a foot from your face, the elephant will suddenly vanish. It will be there one moment and gone the next.

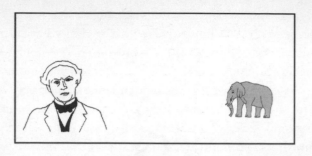

You have just made an elephant disappear into thin air. Well done. Take a bow. Unless you are reading this in a bookshop, of course, in which case demonstrate the trick to the person next to you. (Assuming that they, too, then follow this instruction, soon the whole shop will be doing it.)

This simple illusion works because each of our eyes has a 'blind spot' – a small area inside each eyeball that literally cannot see the world. Rather than tell you that there is something missing, your brain automatically fills in the gaps from the surrounding area, and wipes out whatever is in front of your eyes.

Exactly the same phenomenon applies to the way in which we see the world. Each and every one of us has psychological 'blind spots' that can cause us to miss obvious openings, simple solutions to complex problems and opportunities that could transform our lives.

> ❝ Four things never come back: the spoken word, the spent arrow, the past and the neglected opportunity. ❞
>
> OMAR IDN AL-HALIF, ARAB SCHOLAR

This book shows you how to overcome these blind spots and see what is right in front of your eyes. Along the way, we will discover how spotting the obvious has resulted in many major developments in science, industry and business. How it led Newton to understand gravity, and Darwin to develop his theory of evolution. How it inspired Gutenberg to invent the printing press, and the Wright brothers to build the world's first aeroplane. As well as how it helped make Henry Ford a multi-millionaire and countless others to produce many of the world's best-selling products and services. But this little book is not just about changing the world. **The principles described here can be applied on a daily basis to help enhance your personal and professional life. To build business and forge new relationships. To innovate and create. To change the way in which you see yourself and others.**

The ideas described in this book have their roots in my previous research into the psychology of luck. For over ten years I studied the lives of hundreds of exceptionally lucky and unlucky people, and published my findings in *The Luck Factor*. I discovered that some people experience far more lucky breaks and opportunities than others. Why? Because, without realising it, they are able to overcome their psychological blind spots and see obvious opportunities that most people miss.

> ❝ Opportunities multiply as they are seized. ❞
>
> SUN TZU, CHINESE GENERAL AND AUTHOR OF *THE ART OF WAR*

Perhaps the strongest response to this work has been from the business community. Almost everyone has been excited by the idea of being better able to spot and take advantage of unexpected opportunities. This enthusiasm is fuelled by the fact that present-day businesses are operating in more unpredictable – and competitive – environments than ever before. Gone are the days when organisations could predict the future with unerring accuracy and simply assume that there would be a market for their products and services. Instead, a huge increase in the rate of change has created a far more fluid, unpredictable and challenging environment.

> ❝ To improve the golden moment of opportunity, and catch the good that is within our reach, is the great art of life. ❞
>
> SAMUEL JOHNSON, BRITISH WRITER

Opportunities come and go on a daily basis. Just like Houdini's elephant, they will be there one moment and gone the next. Given this ever-changing climate, it is not surprising that businesses are eager to discover how they can gain an edge over the competition by quickly spotting, and making the most of, these opportunities. This book is a response to that wave of interest. It presents new research that builds upon my original work on luck, and describes four simple techniques that can be used to spot unexpected opportunities.

So what has all of this got to do with gorillas? It's a good question. The book's title comes from a 30-second film made by Harvard psychologist Daniel Simons and his colleagues to study the psychology of vision.[1] The film contains six basketball players – three of them are wearing white T-shirts whilst the other three are wearing black T-shirts. The people in white T-shirts have a basketball and, during the film, pass it between one another. Halfway through the film, a man dressed as a gorilla slowly walks on, saunters through the players, beats his chest at

the camera, and then walks off (see the photo on page 4). Volunteers are asked to watch the film and count the number of times the people in white T-shirts pass the basketball to one another. At the end of the film, everyone is asked whether they saw anything unusual. Amazingly, very few people spot the gorilla. It is the perfect demonstration of an unbelievable psychological blind spot.

I have shown my own version of this film in business talks many times over the years. At the end of the demonstration I ask one simple question: 'Did you spot the gorilla?' Most people look at me blankly and so I show the film again, but this time point out the man in the gorilla suit. The reactions are fascinating. Many people are stunned into silence. Some laugh nervously. A few simply refuse to believe their eyes and accuse me of switching films.

A few years ago I showed the film to an audience of eminent scientists. Soon afterwards, one of the country's most distinguished authorities on molecular biology described on national radio how the gorilla had changed his life by making him realise how much he might be missing in his laboratory.

On another occasion I presented the demonstration on BBC television and then interviewed people about their reaction to the film. This is what they said:

'It's amazing, I really would not have thought I could have missed it.'

'Incredible, I mean, really incredible.'

'It makes you wonder what else you are missing in life.'

The gorilla is a powerful and fun metaphor for the psychological blind spots that cause us all to miss the obvious. Seen in this way, this book is all about how to spot gorillas in both your personal and professional life.

Now it is time to grab your binoculars, because we are about to embark on a gorilla-spotting safari that will change the way you see the world forever.

Two quick points before we set off.

Firstly, because you won't want to miss anything along the way, you might want to test your binoculars by trying to find the gorilla hiding among the herd of yet-to-be vanished elephants in the illustration below.

Secondly, I hope you don't mind, but I have invited two friends to join us on the journey.

'Where did you get this from?' asked Oliver.

'A friend recommended it to me,' replied Lucy. 'He said it had really made him think about things and that we should take a look at it – what did you think?'

'Well, to be honest, I only had time to read the introduction, but I had no problem spotting the gorilla among the elephants so if it's all as easy as that, I should produce a new theory of evolution by Wednesday and become a billionaire by the weekend!'

Oliver handed the book back to Lucy. 'Don't get me wrong, I think it'd be great to be able to see obvious opportunities – but I just don't believe the two of us will spot any world-changing gorillas.'

'Well done Oliver, that's the spirit – giving up before you even begin!' replied Lucy sarcastically. 'But it isn't just about changing the world – it's about applying the ideas to everyday life. Look, you were at the meeting last week and heard about all the things that aren't going well in the company. Marketing were struggling to come up with a good idea for the new ad campaign, there were more complaints because the lifts are so slow, no one had any thoughts about how to get people to bond at the conference next month, and the new technology in the warehouse is still not working properly. Maybe it's time to explore some new ways of thinking.'

'Hmm . . . I take your point. It's just that I've never been very good at things that involve being creative, or thinking differently, or any of that kind of airy-fairy stuff.'

'Ah . . . Now we're getting to the root of the problem – well, the ideas in here are all backed up by research, and apparently anyone can use them providing they're willing to give it a go.'

'Okay, okay, you win. What do we have to do?'

'Well, I've heard that there are four main ideas and that the key is to think actively about how they apply to our lives,' said Lucy, picking up a piece of paper and a pencil, 'So, I'm going to make this drawing of a gorilla to remind us to be active rather than passive as we go through the book.'

Lucy folded up the paper, handed it to Oliver and stood up. 'There we go. Could you pin that on the noticeboard for me. I have to go to a meeting with Martha from marketing, but we can talk more about this later. See you.'

'I don't wish to sound sceptical before we've even started, but you're no Michelangelo. Wasn't drawing a gorilla something of a challenge?'

'No, not really – it's just a question of how you look at things,' shouted Lucy as she disappeared out of the office door.

Oliver unfolded the piece of paper, smiled, and carefully pinned it to the noticeboard.

A few moments later he picked up the book and started to read.

CHAPTER ONE

The Primed Mind

In the fields of observation, chance favours
the prepared mind.
Louis Pasteur, French bacteriologist

Before showing people the basketball film, I explain that they are about to take part in an observation test and have to count the number of times the basketball is passed from one person to another during the film. At no point do I mention that the film might contain anything unusual and so nobody expects to see a gorilla. Or, to put it in more scientific terms, people's brains are simply not *primed* to see a man wearing a big silly animal outfit. All of this is vital when it comes to understanding why we miss the obvious. The human brain is often amazingly good at seeing what it wants to observe. When you are hungry, your brain focuses on finding food. When you are thirsty, it looks for liquid. The problem is that your brain can become so focused on seeing what it expects to see, that it misses things that are obvious but unexpected.

You have probably experienced this phenomenon many times in your life. Remember, for example, the time that you were waiting to meet a friend at the railway station, and walked straight past another good friend, who happened also to be there, simply because you didn't expect to see them? Or the time that you tested your binoculars at the end of the Introduction, but, because you were primed to spot the gorilla, didn't notice that all of the elephants had rather unusual legs?

The good news is that it is possible to increase your ability to spot opportunities by using your brain's tendency to see what it wants to see. Have a quick look around you. Perhaps you are in a shop, your office or your home. Wherever you are, look around. Next, choose a colour from the list below:

RED   BLUE   GREEN   YELLOW

Now look around again, but this time focus on any objects that match your chosen colour. If you have chosen blue, just look for blue objects, no matter how small. Perhaps you have now noticed a small blue part of a book cover. Or a piece of blue clothing. Or a tiny patch of blue carpet. When most people do this exercise they report that the scene appears different the second time because they spotted objects, or parts of objects, that they missed the first time. Now choose another colour and repeat the process. Again, look around and only attend to objects, or parts of objects, that match your chosen colour. What did you notice this time? Once again, most people are surprised at how small details leap out at them, and how they notice things that they simply didn't see first time round.

In this exercise, you primed your brain to notice colours and

> What we see depends mainly on what we look for.
>
> SIR JOHN LUBBOCK,
> BRITISH SCIENTIST

objects that you missed when you first looked around. The same concept can be used to spot gorillas. The key is to prime your brain with the types of opportunities that you wish to encounter, or the problems that you want to solve, and then allow it the time and freedom to scan your surroundings for possible openings and solutions. Every day we are bombarded with all sorts of objects, information, meetings, comments, emails, ideas and so on. If your brain is primed to deal with a problem it will unconsciously sift through all of these and quietly work away at the issue. Then, once in a while, it will see a solution, opportunity or opening that it would have otherwise missed. The brain's ability to perform this amazing feat has been demonstrated in several scientific experiments.

In one study,[2] volunteers were asked a series of quite difficult general knowledge questions, such as:

What is the nautical instrument used in measuring angular distances, especially the altitude of the sun, moon and the stars at sea?

The volunteers only answered about 30 per cent of the questions correctly. However, the questions had, without the volunteers realising it, primed their brains to look for the answers in their surroundings. A short while after being asked the questions, the volunteers were presented with a series of words on a computer screen (for example, 'spending', 'dascribe', 'sextant', 'trinsfer', 'umbrella'), and were asked to say whether each was a word or non-word. Although they didn't know it, many of the words (such as 'sextant') were in fact the answers to the questions they had seen previously.

Later, the volunteers returned to the lab and were asked each of the difficult questions again. Amazingly, although they didn't know how or why, this time they answered almost 70 per cent correctly. What the experimenters had done was to prime the volunteers' brains with questions and then present them with an unexpected opportunity to spot the answers to these questions. Had they not been primed by the questions, their brains would not have noticed the relevance of the words that they saw on the computer screen. But, because they had a primed brain, they were able to spot, and make use of, an unexpected opportunity to solve the problem.

In another experiment designed to explore creative thinking, volunteers were shown into a room that had various small objects scattered on the floor and two strings hanging from the ceiling (see the illustration below left).[3] Their task was to tie the ends of the two strings together. There was just one small problem. The length of the strings, and the distance between them, was such that it was impossible to grasp both of them at once. The gorilla-esque solution was to tie one of the objects to the end of one string, and thus convert it into a pendulum that could then be swung towards the other string (see the illustration below right). After the volunteers had worked on the problem for a while, the experimenter would enter the room for a brief chat. On his way out, the experimenter would brush against one of the strings and gently set it swinging. After this, the majority of volunteers thought of the pendulum solution, but were completely unaware that the gently swinging string had acted as an important clue. Unknown to them, their brains had been primed with a problem and so quickly detected, and made the most of, a seemingly chance opportunity.

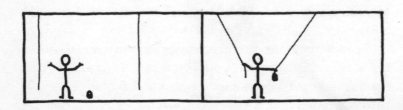

Let's take a short stroll to demonstrate how this works in real life. Imagine going for a walk and passing each of the ten objects in the illustration below.

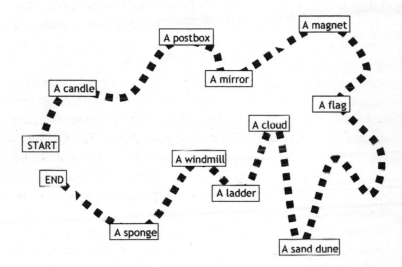

It is quite possible that you didn't really think about the objects as you strolled past them. After all, why should you? They are all everyday items that you will have seen many times before and will come across many times again. This lack of interest is due, in part, to your brain not being primed with a problem. Now we are going to walk around the same route again, but this time you will have a primed brain. Think of a number between 1 and 10 and write it in the box below. You are going to use your chosen number to prepare your brain with a problem. Have a look at the list of problems on page 18 and select the one corresponding to your number.

It is your task to create a new . . .	
1	. . . way of encouraging people visiting shopping centres to put litter in bins.
2	. . . way of building economical housing or offices.
3	. . . way for bookshops to attract customers.
4	. . . type of furniture.
5	. . . way to help employees in a large company have chance meetings with one another.
6	. . . form of public transport.
7	. . . children's toy or game.
8	. . . idea for a film plot.
9	. . . type of outdoor clothing.
10	. . . type of television or radio programme.
11	. . . way of finding children who get lost at a theme park.

Next, spend a few moments trying to solve your chosen problem and write your ideas in the box on page 19. After you have created one or two solutions, stop.

Now we are going to go on the walk again and pass the same ten objects as before. But now allow your brain to become alert and open. Imagine that one or more of the objects will help you solve your problem in a novel, unexpected and simple way. Have a look at each object and spend a few moments thinking about how it could be used to solve your problem. Sometimes you might be able to think of a very literal use for the object. Other times the solution might be based around a concept associated with the object. Once in a while an object might simply spark an association that leads to a completely unrelated idea. Sometimes an object will not lead to any ideas at all – this is fine, in which case simply move on to the next object.

Before you start, it might help if I demonstrate how the idea works. Let's suppose that I had not read the original instructions properly, had chosen option 11, and so was trying to create a new way of finding children who get lost in a theme park. This is a difficult problem because these parks are often very large and lots of lost children are too shy or upset to ask adults and staff for help. As I walk past each of the objects I think about how they might prove helpful. For example, a candle helps people find their way in the dark – why not give each child a specially designed map when they enter the park that clearly indicates where they should go if they become lost. Or, while they are queuing to get in, play them a funny video about a little monkey that once got lost in the park, but was fine because he was sensible and went to the lost monkey kiosk.

On to the next object. A postbox. Okay, well you place letters in a postbox and these are collected and delivered. Why not have boxes all around the park that contain buzzers children can press if they are lost. When a buzzer is pressed, a member of staff can come out and collect the child.

I can't think of anything for the mirror, but a magnet sparks off all sorts of ideas. Magnets attract metal. Let's build the lost person kiosk in such a way that it will catch the attention of children. And now I have come up with a way to reverse the problem. Instead of trying to attract children to the lost person kiosk, let's find out where most children tend to go when they get lost in the park, and build the lost person kiosk there. Okay, now it's your turn. Enjoy the walk and jot down your ideas in the box below.

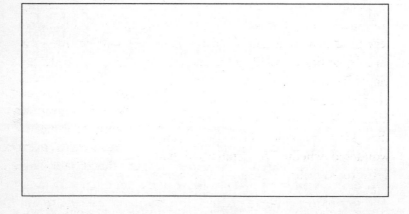

This exercise is a direct analogy of how your brain can operate in real life. The key is not to completely forget the problem, nor to focus your total attention on it. Rather, you need to find the balance – a way of remaining mindful of the

issue but nevertheless being open to the unexpected. Once your
brain has been primed in this way, and been given the time and
freedom to look around, it unconsciously starts to think about
how the events and ideas it encounters
could help solve the problem. Then,
once in a while, it spots a gorilla and lets
you know what it has seen. Suddenly,
you experience that 'aha' moment when
you see an unexpected opportunity or
obvious solution that was right in front
of you. It may seem like an amazing coincidence, an unbelievable lucky break, an inspirational breakthrough or gift from the
gods. In reality, it is a product of a primed brain and open eyes.
A moment of insight produced by a brain that has examined
thousands of possible experiences, solutions and moments, but
has only told you about the one that is meaningful and helpful.

> ❛ People only see
> what they are ❜
> prepared to see.
> RALPH WALDO EMERSON,
> AMERICAN POET
> AND PHILOSOPHER

This simple idea explains some of history's best-known
gorilla-spotting moments. In Ancient Greece, the mathe-
matician Archimedes saw a gorilla in his bath and uttered his
immortal words 'Eureka!' ('I have seen the ape!'). According to
legend, a new king had given the country's best craftsman a
large quantity of solid gold, and ordered him to create an
elaborate new crown. A year later the
craftsman returned and presented the
king with a beautiful crown. However,
the king became suspicious, and
wondered whether the craftsman had
substituted some of the gold with a less
valuable metal. Based on the physics of the day, the king had
correctly worked out that the volume of a pure gold crown
would be slightly less than the volume of a crown that weighed
the same, but contained some less valuable metal. The problem
was that no one could devise a way of measuring the exact
volume of such an odd-shaped object. Eventually, the king

> ❛ I will prepare, and
> some day my ❜
> chance will come.
> ABRAHAM LINCOLN, AMERICAN
> PRESIDENT 1861–1865

turned to Archimedes for help. After thinking about, but rejecting, a few possible solutions, the philosopher decided to take a break and have a bath. As Archimedes slid naked into the tub, the displaced water splashed over the top of the bath and in a flash the solution came to him. Suddenly he came face to face with the gorilla (which, I suspect, was a surprise for both of them). Archimedes realised that if the king's crown were to be placed into a bowl of water, the rise in water level would provide an exact measure of the crown's volume. Archimedes' primed mind instantly recognised an unexpected opportunity to solve a difficult problem.

The same idea also accounts for the creation of some of the world's best-known, and most successful, products. Take, for example, the story behind the invention of the Christmas cracker. In the 1850s, British confectioner Thomas Smith had amassed a large amount of money making and selling the forerunner of the cracker – a cardboard tube containing a sugared almond, paper motto and small trinket. However, Smith's rivals had started to produce similar products, and he realised that he needed a new gimmick to stay ahead of the competition. After considering the problem for several weeks, Smith was standing in front of his fireplace when he kicked a smouldering piece of wood that had fallen from the grate. The log gave off a loud crack and Smith was suddenly inspired to create a cracker that would produce a large bang when pulled apart. In 1860, Smith launched his first 'Bangs of Expectation'. By the turn of the century his factory was producing over 13 million crackers a year, and Thomas Smith had become a very rich man. And all because he spotted a gorilla that happened to fall from his fire.

And Thomas Smith's story is just the tip of the iceberg.

> **The seeds of great discovery are constantly floating around us, but they only take root in minds well prepared to receive them.**
>
> JOSEPH HENRY, AMERICAN PHYSICIST

Consider, for example, how James Watt was struck by the notion of the steam engine while watching a kettle boil. Or how Sir Isaac Newton developed the notion of gravity after seeing an apple fall to the ground. Or how, after a huge amount of careful experimentation, Charles Goodyear eventually discovered a commercially viable form of rubber when he accidentally dropped a sample on a hot stove, and noticed that it formed a highly stable substance. Or how the Kellogg brothers, after striving for years to create a new kind of breakfast cereal, accidentally left some cooked wheat untended for a day, and were surprised to see that it produced a pleasant flaked texture. Or how architect Frank Lloyd Wright played with various designs for the shape of the roof for his church in Wisconsin, before finding inspiration in the shape of his hands at prayer. Or how Sir Alexander Fleming spent years trying to develop more effective antibiotics, and then one day noticed how a small piece of mould had accidentally fallen into one of his petri dishes and killed the bacteria there – an observation that led to him making one of the biggest advances in the history of medicine: the discovery of penicillin.

 I recently conducted a survey in which volunteers were asked two simple questions: 'Do you tend to experience lots of lucky breaks?' and 'If you have worked on a problem for a while, but made little progress, do you tend to stop trying so hard and wait for a solution or opportunity to present itself?'

The results provided strong evidence in favour of the power of the primed mind, with people who frequently experience lucky breaks reporting that they often tended to spend time thinking about a problem, but then took time off, and let their eyes look around and their brain find a solution.[4]

Gorillas are unpredictable animals that come in all shapes and sizes. They might be a person you meet at a party next week. Or an object you see in a shop window. Or an idea you read about in tomorrow's newspaper. Or a comment you hear at a meeting. Or an advertisement you come across in a magazine. Or a talk you attend at a conference. Or a chance remark made by a customer, colleague or child. In fact, there might be a gorilla standing in front of you right now. Or hiding in the undergrowth on your left. Or waiting to pop out from an email tomorrow.

No matter what gorillas look like, or where they are hiding, you will spot them if your mind is primed with a problem, and given the time and freedom to search for solutions and opportunities whenever and wherever they arise.

It is all about being mindful of the problem but not trying too hard.

About seeing more by striving less.

Gorillas are spotted by brains that are prepared, and that are given the time and freedom to search for possible solutions.

Have a primed mind and open eyes.

The practical primate says . . .

By priming your mind with a problem, working on it, then releasing effort and opening yourself up to new and diverse ideas, you enable your brain to come up with innovative solutions.

Hint: To prime your mind with a problem, write down a single sentence that states what you wish to achieve. It might be something in your personal or professional life. Either way, keep it as simple and specific as possible. Next, spend some time and effort exploring possible solutions. Perhaps make some telephone calls, mention the issue to a few people, find the time for some serious thinking, or look for relevant information in books or on the Internet. Then, if you do not come up with an answer, simply stop trying so hard.

Hint: When you release effort, try not to completely forget about the issue, but rather continue to be mindful of the problem. Place a toy gorilla on your desk, or an unusual object in your pocket, to help remind you about it.

Hint: To feed your mind with new and diverse ideas, try going to a museum or art gallery you have never visited before, or flick through an unfamiliar magazine or newspaper, or randomly search and explore the Internet. But don't push it. Simply immerse yourself in novel ideas and experiences, and leave it up to your brain to find connections and create seemingly serendipitous events.

Martha poured Lucy's coffee and smiled, 'So, how's life with you?'

'Oh, you know, same as ever. I'm still redecorating my new flat and going to salsa lessons every Friday. What about you? I heard you're working on a really big ad campaign.'

'Yep, the brief arrived a few months ago, but we're still struggling,' sighed Martha as she picked up a piece of paper from her desk. 'It says, "We need to let people know that the company really cares about building long-term relationships with customers – that we take the long view when others are only interested in making a quick buck." It's a great message but it's so difficult to find something that will really catch people's attention.'

'Hmm . . . I see. Oliver and I have been talking about how we might create change in the company by applying some new techniques that we've heard about. It's all about how to spot opportunities and solutions to problems – would you be on for giving it a go?'

Martha smiled, 'Sure, I love trying new things – in my experience it's usually fun even if it doesn't work. What do I have to do?'

'It's good to hear someone being so open – Oliver was rather more sceptical. Okay, the first step involves thinking about the problem.'

'Believe me, I've done enough of that over the past few weeks.'

'Perhaps you're trying too hard. Apparently it helps if you simply put the problem on the back burner – don't completely forget about it but don't try quite so hard. Just keep your eyes open for ideas and opportunities in unusual and unexpected places, and see what happens.'

'That's fine with me. I did wonder if I was getting in a rut. It's just that when things really matter it's difficult to let go like that.'

'I know, but see what Lady Luck throws at you,' said Lucy reassuringly. 'All you have to do is keep your eyes open for interesting coincidences and experiences that will nudge you in new directions. I'll email you the details.'

'Okay, great. So, talking of new experiences, have I told you my youngest one has just started at a new school?'

CHAPTER TWO

The Power of Perspective

Genius is little more than the faculty of perceiving
in an unhabitual way.
William James, American psychologist

When watching the basketball film, people only see it from one perspective. They believe that it is vital to focus on the ball and so do not consider viewing the film any other way. This is very easy to prove. Ask people to count the number of basketball passes and around 80 per cent of them miss the gorilla. Ask them to watch the film without concentrating on the ball and almost everyone sees the gorilla. Perspective plays an equally vital role in determining what we see when we look at the world, and often dictates whether we spot certain opportunities and openings.

Take a look at the illustration on the following page. There is more to this picture than first meets the eye. In fact, it can be seen in two completely different ways. If you hold the book normally, the illustration shows a rather odd-looking man sitting in a boat by an island, staring nervously at a giant fish. However, if you turn the book upside down, the illustration transforms into a drawing of the same odd man trapped in the beak of a giant bird. This remarkable picture was created at the turn of the twentieth century by cartoonist Gustave Verbeek as a gorilla-esque solution to a rather tricky problem. Verbeek regularly produced four-panel cartoons for *The Sunday New York Herald*, but wanted to present his readers with more elaborate, eight-panel, stories. When newspaper editors refused to allocate more space to his work, he created images that depicted one scene when viewed normally, but another when turned upside down. In this way, Verbeek was able to fit eight-panel storylines into a four-panel cartoon.

But the illustration also relates to gorilla-spotting in another, more profound, way. Very different parts of the drawing are apparent from each of the two viewpoints. When the book is held normally the island dominates the illustration, but when it is turned upside down the island completely disappears. Likewise, when the book is turned upside down the giant bird is obvious, but when it is held normally the bird is almost impossible to spot. The same idea also applies to spotting opportunities. Any event, person, object, product, service, relationship, organisation or situation can be seen in many different ways. From some perspectives it is difficult to see gorillas, whilst from others it is almost impossible to miss them.

Take, for example, the following problem:

How can you add just one line to the following statement in order to make it correct?

$$10 \; \text{T0} \; 11 = 10.50$$

There is a straightforward solution to the problem. However, right now your brain is probably viewing the situation from a certain perspective, and so you are unable to see the gorilla. If you haven't managed to solve the puzzle, and would like a subtle hint, please turn to page 101.

Did that help? When you first encountered the problem, your brain assumed that the statement involved some form of mathematics. Under these circumstances it seems impossible to solve. But once your brain changes its viewpoint, it is much easier to see what has been right in front of you all along. In case you still haven't solved the problem, let me put you out of your misery. The statement is all about time, rather than mathematics. To make it balance, all you have to do is add a short line over the second '1', thus converting the number '10' into the word 'TO':

$$10 \; \text{TO} \; 11 = 10.50$$

Now the equation reads 'ten to eleven is the same as ten-fifty'. From one perspective it is difficult to see the gorilla, whilst from another it is blindingly obvious.

Let's try another problem. Imagine it is your birthday and that you have invited seven friends round for tea. Someone has been kind enough to give you the fruit cake shown in the illustration below, and you want to cut it into eight equal pieces so that you and your seven friends can all enjoy a slice of the action. There is, however, one problem. You only have one knife and it is not very sharp. In fact, it will only cut the cake three times before becoming completely blunt and utterly useless. So, here is the question: Is it possible to cut the cake into eight equal pieces using only three straight cuts? Mark your cuts on the following illustration.

Most people really struggle with this problem. Some cut the cake in half and then give up in despair. Others cut the cake into quarters and then say that the task is impossible. A handful say

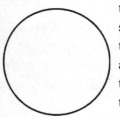

that they could solve the problem by suggesting that it was about time some of their friends went on a diet. In fact, the answer is obvious when you see it from the correct perspective. The illustration on the left encourages you to look down on the cake. Now look at the illustration below, left.

Here the cake is shown in a three-dimensional perspective, and that is the key. To solve the problem, simply cut the cake into quarters, and then make one final horizontal, rather than vertical, cut (see the illustration below, right). The gorilla is obvious when you see the puzzle from the correct perspective.

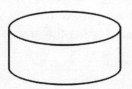
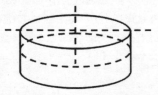

 Being able to see the world from different perspectives often requires an ability to tolerate uncertainty. Psychologists have developed standard questionnaires for measuring the degree to which people are comfortable with ambiguity. These questionnaires contain the following types of questions:

Please circle either TRUE or FALSE for each of the following statements:

I like dealing with problems that have clear-cut answers.	TRUE	FALSE
I don't like breaking rules.	TRUE	FALSE
I believe that there is a clear difference between right and wrong.	TRUE	FALSE
The best part about working on a problem is solving it.	TRUE	FALSE
I believe that most situations are best seen from one perspective.	TRUE	FALSE

In this example, the more times a person circles the word 'FALSE', the higher their tolerance of ambiguity. My research has revealed that people who report experiencing more lucky breaks in life tend to circle 'FALSE' more frequently than those who don't experience such opportunities.[5] This is strong evidence in favour of the link between gorilla spotting and the ability to see the world from many different perspectives.

Don't feel bad if you didn't realise that the equation was all about the time or that the cake could be cut horizontally. After all,

even experts sometimes miss the obvious. At the start of the book
I mentioned the world-famous magician, Harry Houdini. As well
as making elephants disappear, Houdini also earned a consider-
able reputation for being able to escape from some of the world's
most secure jails. He was norm-
ally able to make his escape
within a few hours. However, on
one occasion, he was shut in a cell
and really struggled to pick the
lock on the door. The hours ticked by, and still he couldn't escape.
Eventually, tired and exhausted, he leant against the cell door. As
the door swung open, Houdini realised that he had been trapped
by his own assumptions – the jail warders had left the door un-
locked and he had wasted hours attempting to perform the
impossible by picking a lock that was already open. Houdini's
brain had viewed the situation from just one perspectives and so
had missed a gorilla that would have let him out of the cell within
seconds.

> **Originality is simply a
> fresh pair of eyes.**
> WOODROW WILSON, PRESIDENT OF THE
> UNITED STATES OF AMERICA 1913–1921

Your brain adopts certain viewpoints for a number of
reasons. Sometimes it is due to the way in which you have been
brought up. Other times it is because of the situation in which
you find yourself. Often it is because you find a certain viewpoint emotionally comforting. Once in a while, it is because lots
of other people have adopted the same viewpoint, and you
don't want to be out of the in-crowd. The big problem is that
once your brain looks at the world one way, it finds it very
difficult to see things from any other perspective. Take a look at
the illustration on page 37. I would like you to use a pen or
pencil to make each of the 16 boxes into a different object. So,

for example, you might add a few lines to one box to transform it into a parcel, or change another into a mirror.

Your goal is to produce lots of diverse ideas. This is not a test of your artistic abilities, so please do not spend too long on each box. You have 3 minutes to complete as many boxes as possible.

Okay, away you go.

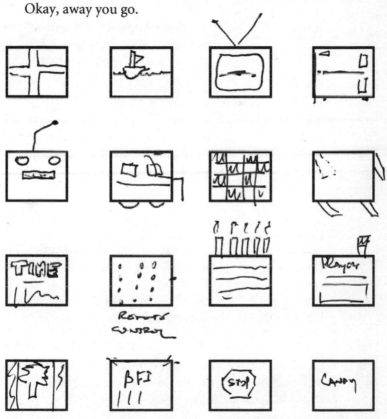

How did you do? Most people find the initial boxes easy but then start to run out of ideas surprisingly quickly. This is because once your brain starts seeing the boxes in certain ways, it becomes progressively harder to view them any other way. On average, most people only complete about nine boxes in 3 minutes. To overcome the problem you have to encourage your brain to adopt many different perspectives. To be more open and fluid, and to keep on twisting and turning the world. It isn't difficult. In fact, it is a little bit like Houdini trying to escape from his jail cell – all you have to do is lean against the door and out you come. Each of the ten suggestions below will help your

1	Imagine that the box is really huge; what is it now?
2	Draw a simple geometrical shape inside a box; what is it now?
3	Imagine that you are a child; how would you see the box?
4	Imagine that the box is something that you would find underwater; what is it now?
5	Imagine that the box is red; what is it now?
6	Imagine that the box is part of a car; what is it now?
7	Imagine that you are an accountant; what is the box now?
8	Imagine that the box contains something explosive; what is it now?
9	Randomly place your finger on one of the words listed below. How can this word be used to create a new and original way of looking at the box? Diet Television Iceberg Flea Bed Ship Advertisement Hand Rock Chimney Hair Crown Glasses Train Japan Baby Clay Bear Violin Pizza Chemistry Snake Necklace River Unicycle
10	Repeat Step 9, but select a different random word.

brain see a box from a new perspective. Try using the suggestions to complete some of your blank boxes and see what happens.

How did you do this time? When people apply the suggestions they often find it quite easy to produce lots of additional boxes. The illustration below contains some of the more creative boxes that people have produced when completing this task.

Man in prison	Mouse hole	Tent	Tea bag
Playing card	Wall	Tray	Person in car
Mug of coffee	Kennel	Flag	A vote
35mm film	Envelope	Pyramid from above	Calculator
Bed from above	Cat flap	Football pitch	Drawers
Earth from space	Block of wood	My mind!	Cinema

But there is more to gorilla spotting than just changing perspectives. Look at the illustration below and imagine that it is a large sandpit. Now imagine that someone has randomly chosen a place in the pit and buried some money there. You have just one opportunity to dig down and try to find the buried money. Without thinking about the problem too much, simply place an 'X' in the box to indicate where you would dig. We will return to your chosen location shortly.

> Don't think you're on the right road just because it's a well-beaten path.
>
> ANON

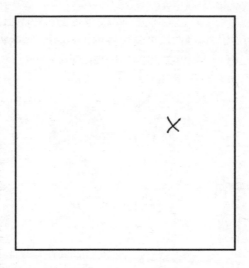

Humans, like gorillas, are group animals, and often lots of people are trying to spot the same opportunities and solve the same problems. Unfortunately, we all have the same type of brains, have been brought up in roughly the same way and watch the same films and television programmes. Because of our collective minds and shared experiences, we all tend to think alike. For example, in the previous chapter I asked you to choose a number between 1 and 10. Most people select the number 7.[6] On page 38 you were asked to draw a simple geometrical shape inside one of the boxes. Most people draw a circle. What has this got to do with the imaginary sandpit and buried money? Well, when it comes to looking for opportunities, we all tend to look in exactly the same places. I have asked hundreds of

> Let your hook always be cast in the pool where you least expect it; there will be the fish.
>
> OVID, ROMAN POET

people to complete the sandpit task. Interestingly, the vast majority of them decide to dig down in the same, rather limited, area (as shown in the illustration below). That is all well and good if you are the first to dig there, but if not, you will fail to find the money because others will have already explored these areas. In fact, you will have a much greater chance of being successful by standing apart from the crowd and looking somewhere new and unusual.

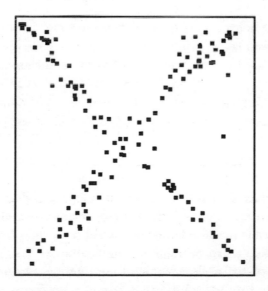

Without realising it, the same type of conformity affects all of our thinking and behaviour. When people complete the boxes exercise they tend to come up with the same ideas again and again and again. Tables. Books. Fish tanks. Picture frames. Televisions. In fact, it is very rare for someone to produce something truly original, or to find a perspective that no one else has ever thought of before. And so it is with gorilla-spotting. When lots of people have considered a problem before, or are trying to solve the same problem right now, they all tend to think in the same way. Gorilla-spotting often requires an original perspective.

 Think of a number between 1 and 50 that contains two odd digits, but not the same odd digits. For example, the number could be 15, because it has two different, odd digits, but it couldn't be 11, because both digits are the same.

Psychologists have asked many people this question. The vast majority choose either 35 or 37. However, people who report experiencing lots of lucky breaks are different – they come up with more unusual choices, such as 17 or 31. In fact, about 60 per cent of people who do not report experiencing lucky breaks tend to choose either 35 or 37, compared to just 40 per cent of people who do spot unexpected opportunities. The same pattern has emerged when I have presented the same people with the 'complete the boxes exercise' described on page 37. People who report experiencing lots of lucky breaks complete more boxes, and produce far more original responses, than those who don't experience such opportunities.[7] All of this supports the notion that spotting unexpected opportunities and simple solutions to complex problems involves being able to see the world in new, unusual and original ways.

Seeing a situation in a new and original way has helped many people spot gorillas over the years. For example, in 1784, Benjamin Franklin was serving as US minister in Paris and, like many other officials of his day, was concerned that Parisian shopkeepers were having to spend very large amounts of money on candles because in winter they were open for business during the early hours of darkness. There are many ways in which he could have approached the problem. He could have suggested cheaper ways of making candles, or come up with more efficient candles that burnt both brighter and longer than existing ones. But he didn't. Franklin removed the blinkers from his brain, looked at the problem from a totally new viewpoint and spotted a gorilla. After much consideration, he suggested that if the whole country altered their clocks twice a year the shopkeepers would use far fewer candles because their opening times would coincide with greater periods of daylight. Many others had tried to solve the problem before Franklin, but had simply assumed that it wasn't possible to alter time. His suggestion initiated the notion of Daylight-Saving Time – an idea that has helped save huge amounts of energy, and countless lives, throughout the world.

> To succeed, jump as quickly at opportunities as you do at conclusions.
>
> BENJAMIN FRANKLIN, AMERICAN STATESMAN AND SCIENTIST

The same type of thinking has also played a key role in business. Time and again, new products and services have been created by people who have been able to see the world from a fresh perspective. Take, for example, the discovery and development of one of the most successful paper products of all time. During the early 1980s, a research team working at 3M were attempting to develop a really strong adhesive. However, all

> Ability is nothing without opportunity.
>
> NAPOLEON BONAPARTE, MILITARY COMMANDER AND EMPEROR OF FRANCE

did not go according to plan, and instead they ended up with a substance that was extremely weak. Any paper coated with this substance became only slightly sticky, and could be easily be peeled away from other surfaces. Most researchers would have confined the product to the bin. After all, they had found the exact opposite of what they were looking for. But one team member looked at the situation in a new way. Rather than trying to find a solution to the original problem, why not find a problem to the new solution? This simple idea turned the whole situation on its head and focused attention on finding an application for slightly sticky paper.

After thinking about the issue for a while, one of the team attended a church service and became somewhat frustrated when the scrap of paper that he was using as a bookmark fell out of his hymnbook. He quickly realised that the new adhesive could be used to create a bookmark that would be sticky enough to remain in the book, but not so sticky that it couldn't be easily removed. Eventually 3M realised that the new product had applications far beyond bookmarks, and so started to produce pads of paper that could be stuck and removed at will. Post-its® became a huge hit, and each year tens of thousands of related products are now sold throughout the world.

And it is not just about Parisian shopkeepers and semi-sticky paper. Seeing the world from an original perspective, and looking for opportunities in places that others avoid, has uncovered countless gorillas over the years. Consider how some businessmen in the 1940s came across a few ranches in the middle of a desert and saw the opportunity to create the billion-dollar industry that is now Las Vegas. Or how the Wright brothers solved the problem of manned flight by building an aircraft that soared like a condor, rather than following in the footsteps of their

> Whenever you find yourself on the side of the majority, it is time to pause and reflect.
> MARK TWAIN, AMERICAN NOVELIST

predecessors and trying to mimic the rapidly flapping wings of a sparrow. Or how Charles Darwin turned conventional thought on its head by seeing a gorilla, realising that it resembled a human, and producing his theory of evolution.

Gorilla-spotting is about seeing the same situation, problem or event from several perspectives. It is about not accepting the first viewpoint that comes along, but exploring different ways of looking at what is right in front of you. It is about questioning assumptions and removing blinkers. About not being trapped by context, past experience or your emotions. It is about looking at the situation from above and below. Forwards and backwards. It is about resisting being critical, and so generating lots of ideas. Producing other solutions when you think that you already have the answer. Finding a perspective that few others will take. It is about fostering innovation and originality. Using a novel analogy to see a situation in a new way. It is about looking where other people don't look. Breaking the fucking rules or not knowing them in the first place. Being random and having fresh eyes. Avoiding the centre of the sandpit and digging at the edges.

Most of all, it is about seeing the world for the very first time.

The practical primate says . . .

Changing perspectives is a powerful tool in the search for gorillas – explore as many ways of looking at the situation as possible.

Hint: Whenever you have an important problem to solve, get an A4 sheet of plain white paper and a pen. Now, cover every part of the paper with possible solutions from many different perspectives. Value quantity over quality, originality over tradition, and enjoy the sense of ambiguity created by looking at the issue from new and exciting viewpoints.

Hint: Finding it difficult to see the problem and possible solutions from lots of different perspectives? Try using some of these techniques:

- How would a child, a complete idiot, your closest friend, an artist, an accountant, a musician and a chef approach the problem?
- Think of two analogous situations by applying the 'is like' rule (e.g., attracting more people to my business *is like* a street entertainer trying to attract a crowd). How is the problem solved in these situations? Does this help you see a novel solution to your problem?
- Draw a diagram or use numbers to express your problem in a new way.
- Remember how researchers solved the 'non-sticky glue problem' by changing the problem. How can you change your problem?
- Look at the solutions you have generated so far – what assumption are they all making? Think the unthinkable by questioning that assumption.

- Think about solving the problem by doing the exact opposite of every solution you have listed so far.

Hint: When you come up with what appears to be a great gorilla-esque solution, imagine that it is impossible to implement and generate two more ideas.

Gorilla-spotting involves turning the world upside down and standing alone rather than running with the crowd.

Find new and original perspectives.

Oliver finished writing on the poster and turned around to see Lucy quickly thrusting a few files into her bag.

'Oliver, if you don't hurry up we're going to be late for the meeting.'

Oliver looked surprised. 'What are you talking about? We don't have to be there for another 10 minutes.'

'That's right. But the meeting is on the top floor – it's too far to use the stairs and the lifts are really slow here, so we have to allow extra time.'

'Sorry, you're right – I forgot.' Oliver started to collect papers from his desk.

Lucy quickly walked out to the lifts and pressed the 'up' button. A few moments later Oliver arrived, complaining. 'These lifts are such a pain. They aren't just wasting people's time – they also really annoy everyone, including customers. If I had a pound for every time someone had arrived at a meeting in a bad mood because . . .'

Lucy interrupted, 'Hey, I've got an idea! Instead of focusing on the problem, why don't we talk about possible solutions. Let's use some gorilla-spotting techniques. We need to come up with lots of different ways of looking at the issue. I'll kick things off – we could move buildings.'

'Nope, that won't work – far too expensive.'

'I don't think you're supposed to be critical, just generate ideas,' retorted Lucy.

Oliver looked puzzled. 'But you're criticising me now.'

'That's different. You deserve it. Come on, let's try some other perspectives. We could spend loads of money installing another lift or making these ones faster. Or cut down on the number of people using them.'

'And how on earth would we do that?'

'Oh, I don't know. Perhaps we could stagger when people arrive and leave for work. Or we could put the smaller departments on the top floors so fewer people are going up there. Or get people to use the stairs more by paying them or donating money to charity for each step they take. Or promote fitness in the company by having posters pointing out the cardiovascular benefits of using the stairs and how many calories are burned per floor.'

Oliver suddenly looked excited. 'I can see it now! "A gym between every floor". Or, you know Eric Heaven who works in accounts – we could move him to the top floor and have a poster saying "Take the stairway to heaven".'

A sudden 'bing' announced the arrival of the lift, and Lucy and Oliver quickly walked inside.

'I know,' said Oliver. 'We could make that binging noise even more annoying so that people really don't want to take the lift.'

Bing! The lift arrived at the fourth floor.

Lucy laughed, 'Or we could have the lift only stop at the even floors, and then people would only have to walk a maximum of one flight of stairs.'

Another 'bing' announced their arrival on the eighth floor.

'Or,' replied Oliver, 'we could have a slow lift for people who aren't in a hurry and would like the chance to network with others in the company. I've always thought they should do that with supermarket queues. In fact, the other day I was thinking – we all communicate by email so much these days, we miss out on all those chance meetings that used to happen when people actually walked around the building. Yep, I think that's the best way forward.'

'Careful. We shouldn't fall into the trap of thinking we have the best perspective on the problem – let's keep going with more ideas.'

Lucy and Oliver looked blankly at one another. Bing. The lift doors opened on the top floor, and Oliver and Lucy walked out.

'Here we are – that actually seemed much quicker than normal,' said Lucy. 'I guess we were so busy talking about how to speed up the lift that time went by much more quickly.'

'That's it!' exclaimed Oliver. 'We don't need to change anything. All we have to do is give people something to do while they're waiting for the lift to arrive or while they are in it. We could put a mirror outside so they could check they look okay. Or we could put a TV on each floor. Or have some nice artwork for them to look at. Or hang up some advertisements about our new product lines. Or have a message board inside the lift. Anything to keep folk occupied and interested.'

'You know, for someone who was sceptical about this whole thing, you're getting surprisingly good at gorilla-spotting.'

CHAPTER THREE

Playful Matters

We do not stop playing because we grow old. We grow old
because we stop playing.

Anon

When I show the gorilla film I sometimes ask people to simply
count the number of basketball passes. Other times, I present
people with the same instructions, but use various techniques to
place them under just a little bit more pressure. For example, I
tell them that counting the basketball passes is both important
and difficult. Or say that the film will be used to test the
observational skills of men versus women. Or that it is a
competition between one side of the room and the other. Or
managers against their staff. Whatever the wording, the results
are always the same – when people feel under even the slightest
pressure, far more of them miss the gorilla.

Why? Well, when your brain becomes stressed it focuses its
attention into a tiny area, rather than stepping back and seeing
the bigger picture. Your brain becomes so anxious to see what

it thinks is important that it forgets to look around and, in doing so, often fails to spot passing gorillas. In fact, sometimes even the most obvious solutions can literally go right over people's heads. Many years ago, I used to work as a professional magician and one of my favourite magic tricks was a brilliant illustration of the relationship between pressure, attention and missing gorillas. The trick is usually performed in front of a small audience. A volunteer is invited on stage and asked to sit on a seat facing the audience. The magician stands next to the seated volunteer and rolls a paper napkin into a ball. He then asks the volunteer to watch closely. The volunteer is usually fairly stressed because they are suddenly sitting in front of lots of people and having their observational powers put under the microscope. The magician places the ball carefully into his closed fist and asks the volunteer to imagine that the ball has disappeared. When the magician opens his hand, the volunteer is amazed to discover that the ball has indeed vanished. The audience is also amazed. But not at the disappearance of the ball. Instead, they are amazed at the reaction of the volunteer. Why? Because everyone in the audience has seen exactly how the trick was performed, but is amazed that the volunteer didn't notice what was happening. The secret is simple. As the magician pretended to place the ball into his closed fist, he simply flicked it straight over the head of the volunteer. The audience saw the ball fly into the air and land on the stage behind the volunteer. Because the volunteer was focused on the magician's hands he didn't see a thing. The audience was looking at the bigger picture and saw exactly what happened.

But why do we tend to become focused when we are stressed? Once again, it is all down to how your brain works. If you could open up your skull and look inside you would see a brain of two halves. A left hemisphere and a right hemisphere. Although these two parts of the brain look identical and work together much of

 For the past ten years I have been studying why some people are consistently lucky and others unlucky. In one study, I gave people a newspaper, and asked them to look through it and tell me how many photographs were inside.

What I didn't tell them was that halfway through the newspaper I had placed an unexpected opportunity. This 'opportunity' took up half of the page and announced, in huge type, 'Win £100 by telling the experimenter you have seen this'.

The unlucky people tended to be so focused on the counting of the photographs that they failed to notice the opportunity. In contrast, the lucky people were more relaxed, saw the bigger picture and so spotted a chance to win £100. It is a simple but persuasive demonstration of how lucky people can create their good fortune by being especially good at spotting gorillas.

the time, they have quite different ways of seeing the world. Neuro-psychologists have devised a very simple way of demonstrating the contrasting ways in which the hemispheres see the world.[8] Take a look at the illustration. First of all, focus in on the Ts in the illustration on page 58. Now step back and look at the big H. Neurologists have monitored people's brain activity whilst looking at the Ts and the H. When you were focusing your attention on the Ts your left hemisphere was especially active. However, when you took a step back and saw the big H, your right hemisphere jumped into action. Your left hemisphere is serious and analytical, focused and systematic. Your right hemisphere sees the bigger picture and enjoys a good laugh. By being relaxed and playful you can engage your right hemisphere and so increase the likelihood of seeing the bigger picture.

```
         TTT              TTT
         TTT              TTT
         TTT              TTT
         TTT              TTT
         TTTTTTTTTTTTTTT
         TTTTTTTTTTTTTTT
         TTT              TTT
         TTT              TTT
         TTT              TTT
         TTT              TTT
```

But stress and pressure do not just cause your brain to miss the bigger picture. When your brain becomes stressed it also becomes far less able to see the world in new and original ways. This is easy to demonstrate. In one experiment, I asked people to complete the boxes exercise described in the previous chapter in two quite different situations. In the first situation they were told that they had 3 minutes to complete as many boxes as possible. In the second, everyone was told that they only had 1 minute. In both situations they were stopped after just 1 minute.

Despite having the same amount of time, the results they produced were dramatically different. The illustrations on the following page are typical of the drawings made in the experiment.

This set of boxes was produced by the group told that they had 1 minute:

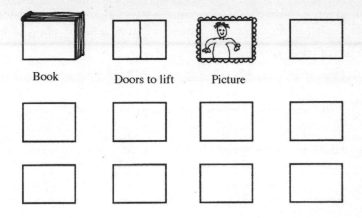

And these were produced by those told that they had 3 minutes:

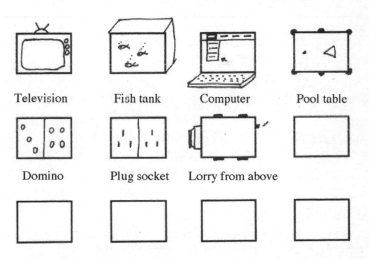

Pressure makes people produce fewer, and less diverse and original, ideas.

The relationship between play and perspective can be easily illustrated with a few lame jokes. From Aristotle to Freud, and from Plato to Wittgenstein, jokes have received some serious attention from many of the world's greatest minds.[9] There is now general agreement that jokes make us laugh because they suddenly confront our brains with new and surprising perspectives – revealing the gorilla that has been standing in front of us all along.

Sometimes it is about the way we view words:

I said to the gym instructor, 'Can you teach me to do the splits?'
He said, 'How flexible are you?'
I said, 'I can't make Tuesdays.'

Other times it is about relationships:

I've been in love with the same woman for 55 years – if my wife finds out, she'll kill me.

And once in a while a joke even suggests a gorilla-esque solution to a problem:

Two boys are walking through the woods when they suddenly see a bear charging towards them. The first boy removes his boots and begins to put on his running shoes. The second boy laughs and says, 'Why bother changing your boots, you can't outrun a bear.' The first boy replies, 'I don't have to outrun the bear, I only have to outrun you.'

The idea is simple – normally our brains place barriers between ideas, categories and concepts. But being relaxed and playful helps your brain start to connect distant ideas. You start to see situations from different perspectives. You create. You see the unexpected.

> ❝ Wit is the sudden marriage of ideas which, before their union, were not perceived to have any relation. ❞
> MARK TWAIN, AMERICAN NOVELIST

Time for a few gorilla-esque puzzles. These are rather odd, but fun, picture-word puzzles that suggest common phrases. For example:

YOU   JUST   ME

represents the phrase 'just between you and me'. Now that you have the general idea, try these four:

MIND
MATTER

R | E | A | D | I | N | G

TIMING TI-MING

THE GORILLAS MIST

Just in case you haven't solved them yet, the answers are 'mind over matter', 'reading between the lines', 'split-second timing' and 'gorillas in the mist'. These types of puzzles have been used by psychologists to study the impact of taking a break on gorilla-spotting.[10] In several experiments volunteers were presented with lots of these puzzles and asked to try to solve as many as possible. They were then allowed to relax for 15 minutes, after which they were shown the puzzles that they had failed to solve first time round and asked to try again. Amazingly, the volunteers now managed to solve over a third of the puzzles that had defeated them just a few minutes previously. The volunteers had not been consciously working on the problems when they were relaxing, instead, the simple act of walking away from the problem and returning at a later date helped their brains see the puzzles in a new and helpful way.

 During my research I asked people to rate the extent to which they agreed or disagreed with the statement 'I tend to adopt a relaxed and playful attitude towards life'. Those who reported experiencing a large number of lucky and unexpected opportunities agreed with the statement far more than those that did not experience so many chances. Also, just for fun, I asked people to rate the extent to which they found the following joke funny:

A dog walks into a telegram office and says: 'Hi, I would like to send the following message "Woof. Woof. Woof. Woof. Woof. Woof. Woof. Woof. Woof."'

The clerk politely replies: 'Did you know that you could send another Woof for the same price?'

The dog looks confused and says, 'Don't be silly, that wouldn't make any sense.'

People who experienced lots of lucky breaks found the joke much funnier than others.[11] All of this underlines the important role that a playful mind-set plays when it comes to spotting gorillas.

Being playful, relaxed and taking a break releases us from the problems of pressure. We see the bigger picture. We explore and imagine. We play with perspective and become original. We have fun. The result? Gorillas hear the laughter and come over to join the party. Relaxed and playful minds have attracted gorillas throughout history. Remember the 'vanishing elephant' illusion that you performed at the start of the book? The idea behind the illusion was originally devised in the seventeenth century as a way of entertaining courtiers during dull speeches. Instead of making an elephant vanish, the same technique was used to give bored courtiers the impression that the speaker's head had disappeared. To perform this version of the illusion the courtiers surreptitiously closed their left eye and focused on a point to the left of the speaker with their right eye. If the conditions were correct, the speaker's head appeared to vanish completely. And it isn't just about vanishing heads of state.

The same idea was also responsible for perhaps the greatest invention of the entire Renaissance. In the fifteenth century, books were produced by a slow and laborious technique that involved hand-carved wooden plates, inking the plates and then pressing each sheet of paper against them. Johannes Gutenberg wanted to revolutionise printing by creating a more effective technique for mass-producing books. He had thought about the problem for a long while, and had already come up with the notion of movable type, but could not find an effective and efficient way of pressing the paper against the type. Whilst visiting a festival celebrating the wine harvest, Gutenberg noticed how a wine press was used to remove the juice from grapes, and realised that the same idea could be used to press paper against his new form of type. Voilà! The birth of the printing press. And all because Gutenberg took time out from his work and visited a wine festival.

The history books show that the same type of playful attitude has also helped spot gorillas in business and industry. Take, for example, the discovery of nylon. When nylon stockings were first made available to the public they became an instant success, with over four million pairs being sold within hours of them going on sale. In addition, the discovery of this remarkable material paved the way for many other related products, including microfilm, audiocassette tape and compact discs. But what played a crucial role in the discovery of nylon? Fun. Du Pont had employed one of the world's leading organic chemists to devise a way of creating synthetic materials that possessed the same properties as silk. Unfortunately, the resulting materials were simply unable to match the strength and appearance of natural silk. Discouraged by their findings, the research team decided to help keep their spirits high by holding a competition to see how far they could stretch some of their newly developed materials. They took a spoonful of one of their latest substances, attached one end to a glass rod and started to pull. The material proved surprisingly elastic and amazed everyone by stretching right across the laboratory. More importantly, when stretched to its extreme, the substance suddenly seemed to change in structure and take on a fine, silky appearance. This simple, and totally unexpected, observation set off a chain of events that resulted in the creation of nylon. A few scientists played at work, spotted a gorilla and changed the world.

And how was the world famous Frisbee invented? Well, an enterprising Yale student once decided to have some fun by taking a disposable pie plate from the Frisbee Baking Company of Bridgeport, turning it upside down, and flinging it at a friend. The two of them instantly noticed that the aerodynamic shape of the disc made it incredibly stable over relatively long distances. Perhaps more importantly, they also noticed that throwing the disc to one another was very enjoyable. The idea soon caught on, and today hundreds of thousands of Frisbees are sold each year right around the globe – and all because a couple of students decided to have some fun with an upturned pie plate.

For the past few years, psychologists have been hard at work creating an unusual test to measure people's Playful Quotient (PQ). Their work has resulted in an odd, but highly effective, test. To take part, all you need is your brain, a coin (a penny is about the right size) and a pen. Please look at the illustration on page 65 and circle one of the numbers between 5 and 20. Do not rush your choice. The number that you choose will play an important role in the test. Simply look at the numbers and circle one that catches your eye or seems to have some sort of intuitive appeal.

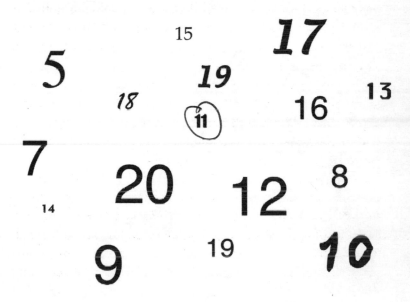

Next, you are going to use your chosen number to measure your brain's level of PQ. The procedure is simple but strange, and involves the type of diagram shown on page 66. The actual diagram we will be using is a few pages away (don't look yet). This first diagram will just be used to illustrate the two-stage process involved in the test.

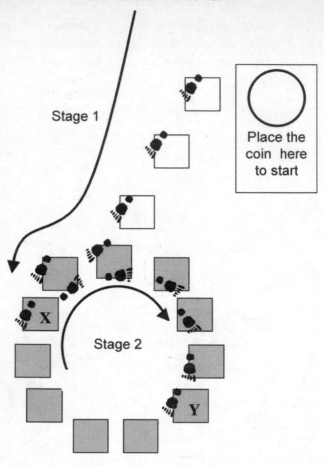

Firstly, you will be asked to place your coin on the box marked 'start', and then count out your chosen number, moving one box each time (when you get on the circle of grey boxes, move anti-clockwise). Let's imagine that a fictitious gorilla is going to test his Playful Quotient, chooses the number 6 and so has landed on the box marked with an 'X'. Secondly, you need to count back the same number clockwise around the circle of grey boxes until you come to rest on a box. In this example, the imaginary gorilla has counted 6 boxes back, and so finished up on the box marked with a 'Y'.

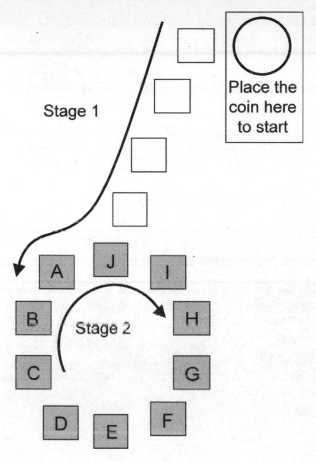

Stage 1

Place the
coin here
to start

A J I

B Stage 2 H

C G

D E F

Now you understand the instructions, it is time for the
actual test. Please place your coin on the circle at the top of the
diagram. Next, move the coin along the boxes, and anti-
clockwise around the circle of boxes, counting out your chosen
number as you go. Then move the coin clockwise back around
the circle of boxes, again counting out your number.
Your coin will now be covering a letter. Please write this letter
on the line below.

This letter reveals a great deal about your brain's PQ. To find out more about yourself, simply look up your letter in the table.

PQ Results Table	
A	Dull, you are no fun at all.
B	You know very few funny jokes.
C	You do not like to enjoy yourself.
D	You rarely laugh and have a below average sense of humour.
E	Your brain is amazingly playful and has a very high level of PQ. This is the best letter to land on by far.
F	The only way of getting a smile from you is to place a coat hanger in your mouth.
G	You don't like having egg on your face and rarely get the yolk.
H	You have got to be kidding. This is the worst one to land on.
I	You don't like laughing because of a strange childhood experience with a clown.
J	People who land here tend to be slightly odd. Am I right in thinking you have lots of dreams about fish?
K	There is no 'K', how did you end up here?

As you may have worked out by now, this is not a serious test of PQ. Instead, the test is based on a simple, and somewhat curious, mathematical principle that ensures everyone lands on the letter 'E'. Sorry about that. Interestingly, once people are classified as having a high PQ score they often are reluctant to explore alternative ways of looking at the test. However, if people misread the instructions and so end up having a somewhat less than positive classification, they study the test in great detail and quickly work out what is going on. It is a great example of how seeing what you want to see makes us reluctant to explore alternative ways of viewing a situation. But enough of this seriousness. The main point of the test is to make you laugh. Hopefully you will show it to others and they will laugh too.

The most significant part of the fake PQ test is how you react to it; those who find the whole thing rather amusing do actually have a playful mind-set. And when it comes to gorilla-spotting, this is as vital as it is enjoyable.

The practical primate says . . .

When you are being too serious your brain becomes constrained. Gorilla-spotting is about jump-starting your right hemisphere into action by stepping back, relaxing and having some fun.

Hint: Spend some time away from the detail. Step back from the situation and use broad brush strokes to paint the big picture. Think about how everything fits together, where it's all heading and what's the point.

Hint: To help relax, take a break for 15 minutes, lie on the grass and just watch the clouds drift by, take a deep breath, book a massage, arrange to go for a quiet walk at the weekend, take it easy and remember to keep everything in perspective.

Hint: Force your face into a smile (or, failing that, force someone else's face into a smile), watch a film that makes you laugh (try Danny Kaye in *The Court Jester*), ask a colleague to complete the Playful Quotient test (but don't tell them that the outcome is fixed), try to incorporate the words 'cheese' and 'pie' into your next meeting or telephone call without laughing, digitally alter a photograph of your colleague so that he or she looks more like an owl, imagine what it would be like to spend the rest of the day dressed in a big furry animal suit.

Being playful and having fun helps people spot gorillas by seeing the bigger picture, adopting new perspectives and being original.

Be seriously playful.

Lucy breezed into the office and sat down at her desk. 'Good morning Oliver, and how are you this fine Monday morning?'

'I'm very well. And you?'

'Good. So, what's on the agenda for today?'

Oliver glanced in his diary. 'Well, first up we have the brain-storming meeting about next month's sales conference. This is the one and only opportunity for our regional sales people to meet one another, and we have to come up with ideas to help break the ice.'

'Oh that's right. I remember this coming up before and no one having any ideas. Good. Just one quick question – why have you got a clown's mask tucked under your arm?'

Oliver looked slightly embarrassed. 'Errr . . . I wondered if you'd notice. Over the weekend, I read the bit in the book about being playful, so I bought the mask from a fancy dress shop. I thought it might help at the brainstorming meeting.'

Lucy raised an eyebrow and laughed, 'So you're going to do a clown act to help things along – great idea.'

'No, I just thought the brainstorming might be more productive if I injected some fun with the mask and these jokes I downloaded from the Internet.'

'I really don't think that's what the book meant when it talked about being more playful,' said Lucy, looking somewhat concerned.

Oliver stood up, put the clown's mask on and looked down at his pad. 'Now who's being the sceptic? Look, how do you know if there is an elephant hiding in your fridge? To get to the other side. No, hold on a moment, that's wrong.'

Lucy laughed and then suddenly stopped. 'Actually, you have given me an idea. The sales people really like jokes – how about we give everyone at the conference a card with either the first line or punch line of a joke on it. Then, they have to go around the room talking to one another until they find the person who has the other half of their joke.'

'It'll certainly break the ice. Also, lots of the wrong com-binations will be odd and funny. Plus it will send out the message that the company is open to new ideas and originality, and we can use the back of the cards for information about sales targets. Also, we can make sure that people are matched up with people from different regions. You're right – it's a great idea – let's suggest it at the brainstorming.'

Oliver looked at his watch and stood up, 'We'd better get a move on.'

'Yep, but before we go into the meeting I think it would be a good idea to take the clown mask off – after all, you don't want to make a complete fool of yourself.'

CHAPTER FOUR

Time to Wake Up

Fish are the last to recognise water.
Anon

In a moment, I am going to name a common object, provide you with a partially complete drawing of the object and ask you to complete the drawing. Because the object is so common, it would be fairly easy for you to locate and therefore make your answer very accurate. However, this is not about your ability to find everyday objects or, indeed, your artistic skills. Instead, it is all about the way in which your brain often fails to notice things that are not only very obvious but also highly familiar. For this reason, please simply complete the drawing on the basis of your memory, rather than actually finding and copying the object. It shouldn't be too difficult. After all, you have seen the object many times in your life. In fact, you saw a drawing of it very recently.

The object is a Roman numeral clock face. The illustration on page 76 shows a partially complete clock face – only the numbers 1, 4 and 10 are missing. Please take a few moments to fill in the missing numbers from memory.

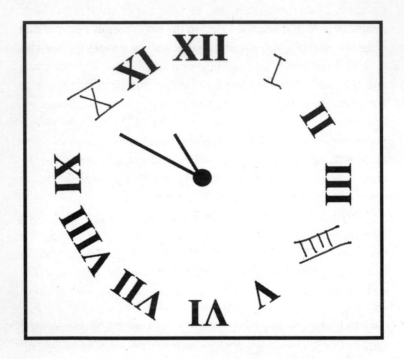

How did you do? To find out, have a look at the illustration on page 101. The important question concerns how you represented the number 4. In Roman numerals the number 4 is always represented as 'IV'. However, on almost all clock and watch faces (with the exception of Big Ben in London) the number is represented as 'IIII'. Despite seeing these peculiar types of clock faces many times in your life, including when you looked at the clue to the puzzle in Chapter Two, you haven't really seen or remembered what is right in front of your eyes.

Let's try another example. This time I would like you to think about an object that you will have seen hundreds of thousands of times. In fact, you probably saw it a few moments ago when you measured your Playful Quotient. The object is a penny. Again, without looking at an actual coin, try to answer the following question. Does the Queen look to your left or your right? Most people believe that she is looking to the left (possibly because that is the way she looks on a stamp) but actually she looks to the right.

Don't feel bad if you didn't do especially well with the clock and the coin. Psychologists have asked hundreds of people to complete these tasks and the vast majority of their guesses are inaccurate.[12] In fact, in some experiments they have shown people a picture of a Roman numeral clock face and asked them to copy it as accurately as possible. Amazingly, even when the clock face is right in front of them, many people still tend to represent the number 4 as IV rather than IIII.

Why is this? After all, you will have seen the coin and clock face many, many times in your life. Well, that is exactly the problem. Your brain is designed to detect change. Once an object becomes highly familiar your brain simply doesn't bother to see what is right in front of you. Thus you do not pay attention to your own currency or stamp because you see them every day of your life; however, when you travel to a foreign country you will tend to look more closely at them because they appear novel and different. This is easily demonstrated. Imagine, for example, that you have just flown into the Gambia and come across the country's postage stamp, shown in the illustration below, for the first time. Straightaway you would spot the gorilla.

The concept is simple. When you come across anything again and again, your brain tends to switch off. It is not that it doesn't see the clock and the coin. Obviously it does, otherwise you would never know how much money you had in your pocket or what time it was. Rather, it fails to examine carefully what it sees. Your brain responds to change, and the clock and coin are exactly the same every day of your life. As a result, your brain switches from manual to autopilot. It ceases to think and starts to assume. It becomes robotic and you become mindless.

> The aspects of things that are most important for us are hidden because of their simplicity and familiarity.
>
> LUDWIG WITTGENSTEIN,
> AUSTRIAN PHILOSOPHER

The same principle applies to every other area of your life. Meet the same people in the same way, day after day, and your interaction with them becomes mindless and mechanical. Tackle the same problems in exactly the same way, soon you stop thinking about what you are doing and simply become a machine. Drive to work along the same route each day and often you cease to remember anything about the journey. Once again, don't feel bad if any of these things happen to you. It is simply a natural consequence of how your brain works. Indeed, it happens to everyone, even people who should know better. William James, one of the founding fathers of modern-day psychology, once famously described how one evening he went upstairs to change before his guests arrived for dinner, but mindlessly followed his usual routine, took off his clothes, put on his pyjamas, and climbed into bed. And what was he working on at the time? Yes, you guessed it, the way in which people's brains sometimes become robotic and unthinking.

The issue is central to gorilla-spotting. Why? Because when your brain is operating in sleep mode, it often fails to see opportunities that are right in front of your eyes. Take a look at the illustration on page 79. This simple street map was used by psychologists carrying out some of the very first research into the relationship between mindlessness and gorilla-spotting.[13] Volunteers were asked to look at the map and draw the shortest route from start to finish. As you will see, there is a diagonal street through one of the blocks, but the direction of the diagonal will not help you get to the finish quickly. Volunteers studied the map and almost all of them marked out various routes using the horizontal and vertical streets.

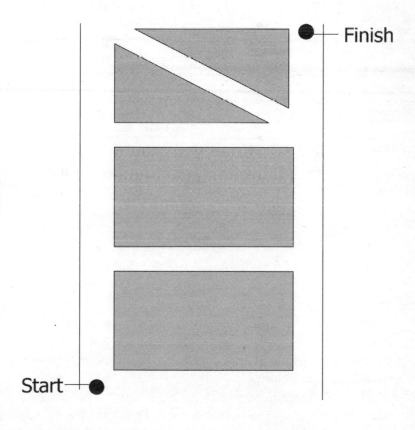

They were then presented with another, very similar map, and asked to complete the task again. In fact, this procedure was repeated ten times. Soon the volunteers became mindless and robotic. Their brains started to fall asleep and, in the same way that people switch to autopilot when they take the same route to work everyday, so they failed to look at what was right in front of them. How do we know this? Because after presenting the volunteers with lots of highly similar street plans, the experimenters did something rather sneaky. They presented them with the map below.

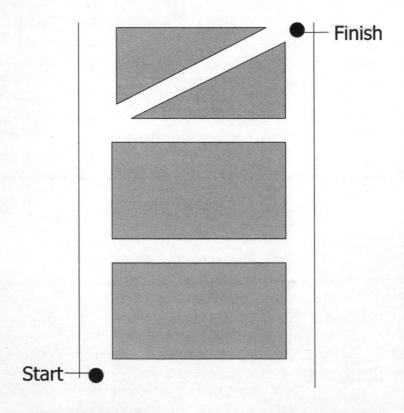

This map differs from the others because the direction of the diagonal street has been changed so that it is now possible to use it to take a short cut to the finish. Almost all the volunteers missed the opportunity. They stuck to the same old routine, failed to spot the gorilla and so kept on taking the long way round.

The problem of mindlessness affects many aspects of our everyday lives. Take, for example, the physics students who were asked how to measure the height of a very tall hotel using only a barometer. Because the students had encountered many such problems before, the vast majority tackled the question by mindlessly thinking about it in a routine and highly familiar way. They explained that it would be possible to measure the air pressure at ground level, travel to the top of the hotel and take a second measurement and then use a complex formula to calculate the height based on the difference between the two measurements. Only one of the students woke up and realised that there was another way of tackling the problem. This student suggested simply going to the hotel concierge and offering to give him the barometer in exchange for him finding out the height of the hotel.

> If you keep doing things like you've always done them, what you'll get is what you've already got.
>
> ANON

Psychologists have become increasingly interested in the concept of 'mindfulness' – the ability to pay attention to the present rather than thinking and behaving on autopilot. Over the years they have developed standard questionnaires to measure this attribute. My research shows that people who experience a large number of opportunities score much higher on these mindfulness questionnaires than those who don't, suggesting that it is easier to spot gorillas if you live in the present and pay careful attention to your surroundings.[14]

This ability to see beyond the obvious can play a vital role in business. Often organisations and individuals within a company do not question routine procedures. Instead, they carry on doing the same things in the same old way, frequently missing an obvious opportunity in the process. Consider, for example, how Henry Ford managed to find a novel way of cutting costs during the production of his new Model T car. Ford insisted that his vendors supply goods to his Michigan car factory in wooden packing crates of a specified size. He even asked them to drill the holes for the screws holding each crate together in carefully specified places. His suppliers assumed either that he was an eccentric millionaire or that the crates were being placed on some form of conveyer belt that could only cope with certain types of crate. Several months later a popular magazine published the real reason for Ford's insistence on certain sized crates. When the wooden crates arrived, Ford's workers were taking out the goods, dismantling the crates and using the planks for the floorboards of Ford's new car. Ford had suddenly realised that it was possible to adapt a highly routine, and very familiar, process and convert it into a new, cost-cutting, opportunity.

So how can the problem of mindlessness be avoided? How can you wake up your brain so that it switches out of auto-pilot and into gorilla-spotting mode? There are two main possibilities.

You can kick-start your brain into being curious whenever you encounter something surprising and unusual. Take a look at the illustration on the next page. Right now your brain will see this as an upside-down image of British ex-Prime Minister Margaret Thatcher. Your brain has seen lots of upside-down faces before and so is somewhat sleepy. It is time to wake up your brain. Turn the book around and look at the face again.

❝ The world will not perish for want of wonders, but for want of wonder. ❞

J.B.S. HALDANE, BRITISH SCIENTIST

The face now appears completely different.

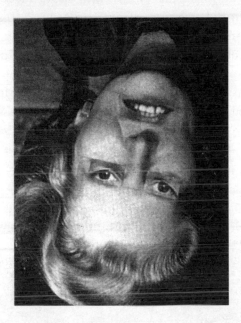

Right now you have a choice. You could treat the illusion as something that doesn't fit in with your understanding of the world and simply ignore it. Alternatively, you can allow the illusion to create a sense of curiosity that wakes up your brain. If you have chosen to adopt the former attitude please skip straight to the start of the next paragraph. The rest of you might be interested to know that the illusion has been created by psychologists carrying out research into facial perception.[15] It works because over the years your brain has been primed to see faces that are normal – that is, faces that have not been digitally altered so that their eyes and mouths are inverted. As a result, when the face is upside down your brain sees what it expects to see rather than what is actually in front of you. Interestingly, the illusion also illustrates many of the other themes that have already been discussed in this book. For example, the illusion is also all about the power of perspective. The face looks one way when the illustration is viewed from one perspective but completely different when seen from another. Also, the use of Margaret Thatcher's face is not an accident; a familiar face seen in an unfamiliar way makes us laugh more than an unfamiliar face seen in an unfamiliar way.

And how about the famous 'vanishing elephant' illusion that you performed right at the very beginning of the book? This illusion was designed as a wake-up call for your brain. You use your eyes all of the time and so seeing is a very familiar process. But the vanishing of the elephant presented your brain with an unusual experience and made it curious about the world. The explanation for the illusion also helps promote curiosity because it reveals just how amazing your eyes actually are. Light enters your eye and hits the retina on the back of your eyeball. Your retina contains over 130 million cells that instantly send information to approximately 1 million optic nerve fibres that connect your eye to your brain. These fibres all exit through the back of the eye via a hole a few millimetres wide, called the optic disk. Since there are no receptor cells in this region, the hole forms a blind spot. However, your brain constantly fills in this blind spot by using surrounding information. In the elephant illusion, you made the elephant fall onto the centre of your blind spot. Your brain then saw the empty space above and below the missing spot, decided that there was probably nothing there and so created an image in which the elephant was no longer present.

And what about the fake measure of PQ described in the previous chapter? As I explained at the time, the test uses a very simple, but rather curious, mathematical principle that results in everyone landing on the same letter. When you discovered what was really going on, did you try to figure out what lay behind this somewhat surprising notion or just pass on by? The same applies to the demonstration involving the Roman numeral clock face described at the start of this chapter. When people take part in this demonstration, some of them immediately try to discover why the number 4 is often represented as 'IIII', whereas others just let this curious phenomenon pass them by without a second thought.

The choice is yours, but the message is simple – whenever you encounter something surprising and curious, you will spot more gorillas if you investigate rather than ignore.

 Scientists have studied the psychology of curiosity for over a century. During this time they have created a wide variety of tests to measure the degree to which people are curious about the world. My research has shown that people who experience lots of lucky breaks and opportunities score much higher on these tests than others.[16] Why is this and what does it mean? Gorilla-spotting is about following up on events and experiences that seem unusual and surprising. It is about asking the 'why?' question rather than walking on. People who are curious are constantly searching for the new and unusual and so encounter far more lucky breaks and opportunities than others.

But there is also another way in which you can wake up your brain. You can get it to switch from autopilot to manual by getting it to look at an everyday experience in a new way. How? By supplying it with interesting and novel information. Take, for example, the computer keyboard. You will have seen such keyboards many times in your life. In fact, there

> I am neither especially clever nor especially gifted. I am only very, very curious.
>
> ALBERT EINSTEIN,
> PHYSICIST AND MATHEMATICIAN

might be one sitting in front of you right now. Now it is time to ask yourself an obvious question that will help you look at this familiar object in a new way. Why are the keys laid out the way they are? In fact, the keyboard was designed in the late 1800s for manual typewriters. The technology of the time was not able to cope with the speed at which touch-typists could hit the keys, and so often they would hit one another and become jammed. The designers came up with a gorilla-esque solution. Rather than spend a fortune trying to improve the technology, they simply created a keyboard where the most common combination of letters (such as 'th' and 'an') were spread evenly apart around the keyboard, thus slowing down typists. They also wanted to create a layout that salesmen who couldn't type could still use to impress clients. How did they do this? By placing the letters needed to produce the word 'typewriter' in the top row, thus making it easy for sales staff to type this word very quickly and impress potential customers. Armed with this new information, your brain will now look at your computer keyboard in a new light.

The same ideas also apply to our everyday behaviour. When we have to carry out the same routine again and again our brains often slip into a type of mindlessness. To kick-start your brain, simply make it believe that it is looking at the world for the very first time. There are lots of ways of doing this. In one experiment psychologists encouraged highly experienced sales staff to approach each client as if they were a totally new person.[17] That is, the staff were asked not to engage in their usual, highly routine sales pitch, but rather to transform a very familiar experience into something new and fresh each time. Customers were asked to rate the sales staff in various ways; the results were remarkable. Switching from autopilot to manual resulted in the sales staff being seen as

> **The less routine the more life.**
>
> AMOS BRONSON ALCOTT,
> AMERICAN EDUCATOR AND
> SOCIAL REFORMER

more charismatic, knowledgeable and persuasive. This straightforward idea woke up the brains of the sales staff and encouraged them to view each and every customer as a potential, and very individual, gorilla.

All of these questions and exercises make your brain active and cause it to look at familiar experiences and objects in a new way. This simple idea has often caused people to spot the obvious. For example, in the early 1950s George deMestral went for a stroll in the countryside in his native Switzerland. When he returned home he noticed that his clothing was covered in tiny cockleburs. Many walkers have experienced exactly the same phenomenon over the years. It was an extremely familiar sight. But George was more curious than most. Instead of merely sitting there, removing them one by one, George asked the 'why' question. He wanted to know why they stuck to his clothing. Close examination soon revealed the cause of the problem – the cockleburs were covered in tiny hooks that easily attached themselves to the loops within fabric. This simple gorilla moment set deMestral thinking. He wondered whether the same idea could be used to attach other surfaces together. This thought eventually resulted in the design and production of Velcro. This incredible material is used in an amazingly diverse range of products, from outdoor clothing to children's shoes, display boards to travel baggage, soft furnishings to space travel.

Gorilla-spotting is all about encouraging your brain to switch from autopilot to manual. It is about being curious and questioning. Noticing the unexpected and wanting to know why. Transforming the ordinary into the extraordinary. Asking the 'why' question just for the sake of it. It is about perceiving each and every moment as if it has never happened before. It is about living in the present as if you haven't seen it all before. It is about breaking routine, and changing habits and habitats. It is about doing things that you have never done before.

Most of all, it is about waking up your brain.

The practical primate says . . .

When the world becomes too familiar, your brain reverts to automatic pilot and stops thinking and noticing. This is when opportunities can be missed. Stimulate your mind and switch to manual.

Hint: Look closely at a particularly familiar object. Perhaps your car. Or the chair that you are sitting in this very moment. Or the pen in your pocket. Or the desk that you have leant on for years. Whatever the object, look at it closely. Look at the texture and colour. Examine it in minute detail. Notice something that you have never noticed before. Right now you are seeing rather than assuming. Notice how this feels. Carry out this exercise whenever you find yourself drifting towards automatic pilot.

Hint: To help become more curious, ask yourself an interesting question each week. It could be anything. Perhaps it is a question related to your work or interests. Perhaps it is just something that you have always wanted to know. Perhaps it will be sparked off by an interesting fact, or an unusual experience, or by switching from autopilot to manual. How do elephants communicate over hundreds of miles? Why do people laugh? Why are bananas yellow? How cmoe yuor bairn is albe to udnertsnad tihs snetence eevn tghouh olny the frist and lsat ltetres of ecah wrod are crreoct? Invest some time and energy into trying to discover possible answers to the question, simply for the sake of finding out.

Hint: Think of someone that you have worked with for years and write down a couple of words to describe that person. These are the main categories that your brain uses to classify them. Now generate alternative ways of seeing them. Think about physical characteristics, their hobbies and interests, the way in which they relate to others, their dreams and ambitions, and the different roles that they play in their life. In fact, anything that encourages you to see them as an individual again.

Be curious. Ask why. Examine the unexpected. Switch from autopilot to manual by making each and every moment the first of its kind.

Be wide awake and curious.

Oliver sat at the pub table and turned to James. 'So, how's life in the warehouse?'

'It's tough at the moment. Basically, we need to be able to have people log the goods in and out, but it's quite cold and dusty down there, so our hand-helds keep on breaking down.'

'Hmm . . . doesn't sound good – what are you doing about it?'

James took out a pencil and began to draw on a beer mat. 'We're doing what we always do – asking consultants to come up with solutions. Their first idea was to find a way of encasing the computers in a kind of airtight casing like this, but the casing quickly became dirty and it was almost impossible to see the display and operate the device.'

Oliver looked at the diagram and started thinking as James continued, 'Then we had another team take a second look, and they came up with the idea of creating a kind of portable, clean room like this that moved around the warehouse with our people inside, but it just wasn't practicable.'

'I can imagine. You know, perhaps we're overlooking the obvious.'

'What do you mean?'

'Well, we tackled the issue by using the same sorts of approaches that have worked in the past – we employed consultants and threw loads of technology at the problem.'

'Sorry, I still don't get where you are coming from,' said James as he placed the pencil back into his pocket.

Oliver smiled. 'Well, it's quite messy in here isn't it – there's lots of smoke and beer on the table, so you wouldn't get your laptop out – right?'

'That's right.'

'So, instead you simply used a pencil – why not have people write with an everyday pencil in the warehouse and then transfer their data to a computer located in a nearby room. The pencil will be very efficient, work in almost any environment, requires no training to use, won't go wrong and it doesn't matter if you drop it.'

James removed the pencil from his pocket and looked at it as if he had never seen one before.

CONCLUSION
It's a Jungle Out There

> Small opportunities are often the beginning
> of great enterprises.
> *Demosthenes, Athenian orator*

And so we have almost reached the end of our journey together. Before we say goodbye, there is time for one final thought. It is estimated that there are only about 650 gorillas alive in the world today. Over time they have become increasingly rare as their habitats and numbers have been, and continue to be, systematically destroyed. And so it is with the type of gorillas that I have been describing throughout this little book.

The world is now a faster and more pressured place than ever before. Yet people are being encouraged to think and behave in the same way as always. To look and see using the same categories and constructs. To conform rather than deviate. To keep to the straight path rather than explore the road less travelled. To fly on autopilot not manual. To accept rather than question. As a result, it has become increasingly important to be able to spot gorillas. To develop minds that are primed and given the freedom to wander far and wide. To view the world in new and original ways. To see the bigger picture by being playful and relaxed. To treat every moment as if it were the first and only. To be curious and so transform the ordinary into the extraordinary.

Gorilla-spotting has already changed the world, and has the potential to further revolutionise both the shape of history and our everyday lives. It can inspire amazing and insightful scientific theories, produce inventions and technology that allow us to live longer and better than ever before, create best-selling products and services, help people forge novel relationships and modify existing ones, and reveal new ways of seeing both ourselves and others. It is as dangerous and radical as it is exciting and necessary. I hope that you enjoyed the trip and spotted some interesting gorillas along the way. Now the safari has come to an end and it is time to return to the real world.

My hope is that it will never look the same again.

'Wow,' said Oliver as he finished writing on the poster, 'and I thought it was just about a guy in a gorilla suit. I must admit, I was sceptical at the start, but it has certainly made me think. The only thing I found slightly annoying was the way the author kept using us as a device to emphasise certain points.'

'Yes, I know how you feel,' said Lucy, 'but apparently it's all the rage in these type of books now. I guess my only disappointment was that Martha didn't come up with a campaign idea about us building long-term relationships with our customers.'

Just then, a quiet pinging sound signalled the arrival of a new email on Lucy's computer.

Lucy looked at the screen, 'It's from Martha and headed "New Campaign Idea".'

'The chances of that!' remarked Oliver, somewhat sarcastically. 'What does it say?'

Lucy opened the email and read it aloud.

To: Lucy Kanzi
From: Martha Washoe
Subject: New Campaign Idea
Hi Lucy,
I just wanted to tell you the exciting
news. You know you suggested I should
take a break from trying to solve the
campaign problem, but keep my eyes open
for new opportunities and see what
happens? Well, I followed your advice. At
the weekend I took my youngest to the new
art gallery that has just opened in the
centre of town.

They had a great exhibition on anamorphic
art. Basically, for centuries artists have
hidden images in drawings by stretching
them lengthways – they look really odd,
until you close one eye and look along the
paper, then suddenly the image jumps out
at you. These pictures were often used to
send secret messages or hide erotic
drawings. To show you what they look like
I have attached one of Charles I that was
drawn in the seventeenth century. Anyway,
as I was strolling around the exhibition,
I suddenly had a great idea for the
campaign. We could get the design team to
create anamorphic drawings of some of our
longest standing customers, and run them
in long, thin, newspaper ads with the
caption 'When it comes to our customers,
we take the long view'.

We could add a line about the person in the picture, along with some text explaining how customers find us attractive because we are here for the long haul, even when times get tough. Also, the whole thing will show that we are creative, willing to be different, and that we really care about our customers because we treat them as individuals and are making them the focus of our ads. We could run the same sort of images in our brochures and even place big versions on posters. The images will be really eye-catching because they will look odd, plus people love showing puzzles to one another, so we have a good chance of reaching a far larger audience than normal.

Anyway, I presented the idea in a meeting this morning and everyone here loves it. I am so excited about this!
Best
Martha

'Perfect,' said Oliver. 'Well, it has to be said, we did manage to spot a few gorillas of our own and it has certainly made a difference around here. Lots more people are smiling since we solved the lift problem. We've saved a lot of money and frustration in the warehouse. Everyone attending the sales conference had a great time getting to know one another and networking. And now Martha has come up with a really wonderful campaign idea.'

Lucy and Oliver held up their coffee mugs and turned towards the poster on the noticeboard.

'To us and our amazing gorilla-spotting abilities . . .' said Lucy.

'And to all of the other gorillas that are sitting out there, right now, just waiting to be spotted.'

As the coffee mugs clinked together a gentle pinging sound announced the arrival of another email.

Oliver looked towards the screen.

'It's a second message from Martha.'

Oliver and Lucy opened the message, looked confused for a few seconds and then laughed.

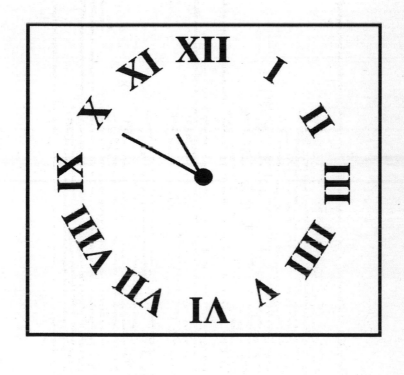

Notes

1. This work is described in Simons, D.J. & Chabris, C.F. (1999), 'Gorillas in our midst: sustained inattentional blindness for dynamic events'. *Perception*, *28*, 1059–1074. A DVD containing the gorilla clip is available from: www.viscog.com. Image reproduced with permission from Pion Limited, London.

2. See Seifert, C.M., Meyer, D.E., Davidson, N., Patalano, A.L. & Yaniv, I. (2002). 'Demystification of Cognitive Insight: Opportunistic Assimilation and the Prepared-Mind Perspective'. In R.J. Sternberg and J.E. Davidson (Eds) *The Nature of Insight*. Cambridge, Massachusetts: MIT Press. Pp. 65–124.

3. Mair, N.R.F. (1970). *Problem solving and creativity*. Belmont, CA: Brooks/Cole.

4. Participants were asked to answer the following two questions on a five-point scale from 1 (strongly agree) to 5 (strongly disagree): 'If you have worked on a problem for a while, but made little progress, do you tend to stop trying so hard and wait for a solution or opportunity to present itself?', and 'I have experienced many lucky breaks in my life.' The Spearman Rank correlation coefficient between participants'

scores on the questions was statistically significant (N=68, Rho [corrected for ties] = .33, p [2-tailed]=.006) indicating that participants who tended to report experiencing more lucky breaks in their life were more relaxed than others. For additional information about this notion, see pp. 48–53 in *The Luck Factor* (Century: London, 2003).

5. Participants were asked to answer the following two questions on a five-point scale from 1 (strongly agree) to 5 (strongly disagree): 'I tend to spot opportunities that others miss' and 'I have experienced many lucky breaks in my life'. In addition, participants were asked to complete the AT-20, a well-known test measuring tolerance to ambiguity. Spearman Rank correlation coefficients between participants' scores on both of the initial questions and their scores on the AT-20 were statistically significant (opportunities; N=114, Rho [corrected for ties] = .40, p [2-tailed]<.0001: breaks; N=114, Rho [corrected for ties] = .30, p [2-tailed]<.002), indicating that participants who tended to report experiencing more lucky breaks in their life were more tolerant to ambiguity than others. For more information about psychological research into the tolerance to ambiguity see: Furnham, A. & Ribchester, T. (1995). 'Tolerance of Ambiguity: A review of the concept, its measurement and applications'. *Current Psychology*, *14 (3)*, 179–199.

6. When researchers asked approximately 200 people to name a number between 1 and 10, just over 30 per cent of them chose the number 7. For more information about this work, and other types of stereotypical thinking, see: Marks, D. & Kammann, R. (2003). *The Psychology of the Psychic*. Amherst, Buffalo: Prometheus Press.

7. Participants were asked to rate the statement 'I have experienced many lucky breaks in my life' on a five-point scale from 1 (strongly agree) to 5 (strongly disagree). They were then asked the 'name a digit' question. On the basis of their

responses to the initial question, participants were split into two groups. Participants (N=59) who assigned a rating of 'strongly agree' or 'agree' were placed into a 'high' group, whilst all other participants (N=39) were placed into a 'low' group. Participants who gave a response of either '35' or '37' to the 'name a digit' question were classified as giving 'stereotypical' answers whilst all others were classified as 'non-stereotypical'. A Chi-Squared analysis revealed a weak but statistically significant relationship between the two variables (Chi-Square [with continuity correction] = 2.73, p [1 tailed] = .05), with the 'high' group giving more 'non-stereotypical' answers than the 'low' group. In addition, participants were asked to complete the boxes task. Participants in the 'high' group completed significantly more boxes than those in the 'low' group (df=96, t-value [unpaired]=2.34, p[2 tailed]=.02).

8. Yamaguchi, S., Yamagata, S., & Kobayashi, S. (2000). Cerebral asymmetry of the 'Top Down' allocation of attention to global and local features. *Journal of Neuroscience, 20*, 1–5. For further information about different hemispheric abilities see: Springer, S.P. & Deutsch, G. (1997). *Left Brain, Right Brain*. New York: W.H. Freeman and Co.

9. For a really witty and engaging review of this work, see: *Laughlab: The Scientific Quest For The World's Funniest Joke* (Arrow, London: 2002).

10. Smith, S.M. (2002). 'Getting Into and Out of Mental Ruts: A Theory of Fixation, Incubation and Insight'. In R.J. Sternberg and J.E. Davidson (Eds) *The Nature of Insight*. Cambridge, Massachusetts: MIT Press, 229–251.

11. Participants were asked to answer the following two questions on a five-point scale from 1 (strongly agree) to 5 (strongly disagree): 'I tend to adopt a relaxed and playful attitude towards life'. The Spearman Rank correlation coefficient between participants' scores on the questions was statistically significant (N=68, Rho [corrected for ties] = .30, p

[2-tailed]=.014), indicating that participants who tended to report experiencing more lucky breaks in their life were also more playful than others. Participants were then asked to rate how funny they found the 'dog joke' on a scale of 1 (very unfunny) to 7 (very funny). The Spearman Rank correlation coefficient between participants' scores on the 'lucky breaks' question and funniness ratings was statistically significant (N=68, Rho [corrected for ties] = −.32, p [2-tailed]=.009) indicating that participants who tended to report experiencing more lucky breaks in their life found the joke funnier than others.

12. For more information on the clock demonstration see: French, C. and Richards (1993). 'Clock this! An everyday example of a schema-driven error in memory'. *British Journal of Psychology, 84*, 249–253.

For additional details on the coin demonstration, see: Nickerson, R.S. & Adams, M.J. (1979). 'Long-term memory for a common object'. *Cognitive Psychology, 11*, 287–307.

13. Rokeach, M. (1948). 'Generalised mental rigidity as a factor in ethnocentrism'. *Journal of Abnormal and Social Psychology, 43*, 259–278.

14. Participants were asked to rate the statement 'I have experienced many lucky breaks in my life' on a five-point scale from 1 (strongly agree) to 5 (strongly disagree), and complete the Mindful Attention Awareness Scale (MAAS). A Spearman Rank correlation coefficient between these two measures was statistically significant (N=98, Rho [corrected for ties]= -.25, p [two-tailed]= .015), indicating that participants who tended to report experiencing more lucky breaks in their life were more mindful than others. For more information on the MAAS, see: Warren Brown, K. & Ryan, R.M. (2003), 'The Benefits of Being Present: Mindfulness and Its Role in Psychological Well-Being', *Journal of Personality and Social Psychology, 84(4)*, 822–848.

15. Thompson, P. (1980). 'Margaret Thatcher: a new illusion'.

Perception, 483–484. Reproduced with permission from Pion Limited, London.

16. Participants were asked to rate the statement 'I have experienced many lucky breaks in my life' on a five-point scale from 1 (strongly agree) to 5 (strongly disagree), and complete the Curiosity and Exploration Inventory. A Spearman Rank correlation coefficient between these two measures was statistically significant (N=98, Rho [corrected for ties]= -.31, p [two-tailed]= .002), indicating that participants who tended to report experiencing more lucky breaks in their life were more curious than others.

17. Reported in Langer, E.J. (1989). *Mindfulness*. Cambridge, Massachusetts: Perseus Books.

Also available in Arrow

THE LUCK FACTOR

Dr Richard Wiseman

The revolutionary book that reveals the four scientific principles of luck – and how you can use them to change your life

For over ten years, psychologist Dr Richard Wiseman has been conducting a unique research project, examining the behaviour of over a thousand volunteers who considered themselves 'lucky' or 'unlucky'. The results reveal a radical new way of looking at luck:

- You hold the key to creating your luck
- There are four simple behavioural techniques which are scientifically proven
- You can use these techniques to revolutionise every area of your life – including your relationships, personal finances and career

For the first time, the elusive luck factor has been identified. Using the simple techniques described in this book, you can learn how to increase your levels of luck, confidence and success.

'These principles can be used to enhance the amount of good fortune people experience in their lives' *Guardian*

'Using Dr Wiseman's scientifically proven techniques, you too can understand, control and increase your own good fortune' *Daily Mail*

arrow books

Also available in Arrow

THE MANY FACES OF MEN

Stephen Whitehead

The book exposes one of the best-kept secrets of all time – What goes on in men's heads?

Ever wondered what a man really thinks when he says 'I love you'? Ever questioned why so many men appear to love their football teams more than their children? Or agonised over whether a particular man can be trusted?

The Many Faces of Men is the first book to lift the lid on masculinity and to disclose the 27 distinct 'types' that make up the male species. In frank and humorous detail, gender expert Dr Stephen Whitehead defines men's inner characteristics and reveals:

- how to predict whether he's a marrying type or a serial seducer
- the telltale signs of an empire builder or a couch potato
- what kind of man makes the best books
- how to spot a poser

Don't live in ignorance of men. *The Many Faces of Men* is an indispensable guide for any woman who wants an insight into the men in her life, or for any man who wants to understand what makes him tick.

arrow books

TRUE BRITS

J. R. Daeschner

When J.R. Daeschner first witnessed cheese rolling, he was astounded. As an American who had lived in the UK for years, he knew the British did some odd things. However, nothing could have prepared him for the sight of men and women – flinging themselves off a grassy cliff in pursuit of cheese. He soon discovered that Britain has scores of seemingly lunatic acts enshrined as traditions: events with strange names like gurning, shin kicking, horn dancing and faggot cutting.

True Brits is the hilarious account of J.R.'s trek around England, Scotland and Wales, as well as a bit of Northern Ireland in London's backyard. From 'Darkie Day' on New Year's Day to the English summer 'Olimpicks' and Pope burning on Bonfire Night, J.R. uncovers the people and places that make Britain great – and at times, not so great.

In his quest to find out why ordinary people do such extraordinary things, J.R. talks to countless characters, catches them in action and even takes part in the events himself. Along the way, he discovers that many of these ancient pastimes provide insights into twenty-first century Britain, including football, francophilia, Page Three girls and Sellafield.

If you think you knew Britain, think again . . .

arrow books

Also available in Arrow

YOUR BACK, YOUR HEALTH

Dr Paul Sherwood

Over ten million Britons suffer from back pain. Many more have other health problems that are caused by their backs. There is little offered to these patients other than temporary relief in the form of drugs, largely ineffective orthodox treatments and complementary therapies. There has *never* been a more permanent solution – until now.

In *Your Back, Your Health*, Dr Paul Sherwood explains his pioneering view of the cause of non-specific back pain and outlines his revolutionary treatment, examining:

- How to identify your pain, understand the cause and deal with it effectively
- Why thousands of hip replacements and disc operations could be avoided
- Why it is essential children's backs are checked frequently
- Why regular back check-ups could dramatically lower your risk of a heart attack
- Your back as the cause of other diseases including migraine, arthritis, indigestion and ME

Dr Sherwood's methods have helped thousands of sufferers from all around the world and are easily adapted for use by other therapists. At last, you can say goodbye to back pain and its related illnesses.

'How to banish backache for good' *Daily Mail*

arrow books

Also available in Arrow

I DIDN'T GET WHERE I AM TODAY

David Nobbs

As a small boy David Nobbs survived the Second World War unscathed, until his bedroom ceiling fell on him when the last bomb to be dropped on Britain by the Germans landed near his home. It was the nearest he came to the war, but National Service woud later make him one of Britain's most reluctant soldiers. It was an unforgettable and often unpleasant experience.

As a struggling writer, David was catapulted into the thrilling world of satire at the BBC when he rang *That Was The Week That Was* with a joke and got through to David Frost, who sent a taxi for the joke. He never looked back. His greatness as a modern comic writer was confirmed by the publication of *The Fall and Rise of Reginald Perrin*, which he adapted into the immensely successful television series that has entered the fabric of British cultural life, through phrases, images and brilliant humour.

A mesmerising, beautifully told tale of a life in writing and comedy, *I Didn't Get Where I Am Today* is the hilarious, poignant and very personal story of David Nobbs' life, which also describes some of the most famous comedians of the last century and captures a golden age of British television.

'He got where he is today by being very funny over a very long period of time' *The Observer*

'Anecdotal, angry, heartfelt and laugh-out-loud funny' *Time Out*

arrow books

Also available in Arrow

A STUPID BOY

Jimmy Perry

From the creator of *Dad's Army* comes the wonderfully written and evocative tale of the life and adventures that inspired the hit TV shows he would go on to create.

Highly entertaining and funny, *A Stupid Boy* provides fascinating glimpses into Perry's *Dad's Army* and his much-loved British comedies, such as *It Ain't Half Hot, Mum* and *Hi-De-Hi!*, and the real-life individuals who inspired the charcacters and events. It also tells behind-the-scenes stories – including how *Dad's Army* came about, and how it was very nearly dropped, never to appear on our screens.

'Charmingly discursive' *Daily Telegraph*

'A naturally gifted popular writer whose feel for character and humour was honed by his own apprenticeship on the stage'
The Times

arrow books

Also available in Arrow

CONFESSIONS OF A REFORMED DIETER

A. J. Rochester

'I love food. Even worse, I love junk food. If lard could be double deep-fried I would eat it. If I could deep-fry headache pills I would. So it's no wonder I'm now the size of a small yet economically viable continent . . .'

When A.J. Rochester is selected to feature in a television series on obesity, she is at first appalled and then resolved. At 109 kilos (17 stone), she knows she needs to lose weight – not because she yearns to become a twiglet but so she can keep up with her little boy and turn her life around at last.

Confessions of a Reformed Dieter charts the highs, lows and plateaus of A.J.'s incredible journey, from overcoming an early setback – waking up in hospital with a broken leg after a drunken binge – to the triumph of shedding the first, and last, kilo.

The result is a funny, insightful and inspiring account of a woman who lost 40 kilos without losing her sense of humour – and discovered a whole new life.

'This month, I read a book that I think will change the life of everyone . . . This is not just a book for overweight people. It's for every woman who looks in the mirror and doesn't like what she sees . . . I found her story brave, honest, instructional and inspiring'
Cosmopolitan

arrow books

RUNNING WITH THE MOON

Jonny Bealby was devastated when his fiancée Melanie died unexpectedly. Two years later and still heartbroken, he took on the challenge of a lifetime. Setting off with only his motorbike for company, he began a daring and dangerous journey around Africa in a desperate attempt to unearth some meaning in his life.

FOR A PAGAN SONG

For a Pagan Song tells the story of how Jonny Bealby traces the paths of his two literary heroes Kipling and Dravot, travelling across remote parts of India and Pakistan and into war-torn Afghanistan.

'Something in Bealby's voice, a mixture of innocence, determination and pain, makes the journey worthwhile. I was glad to be there when [he] reaches his pagan land' *Sunday Times*

SILK DREAMS, TROUBLED ROAD

Whilst in Istanbul investigating the possibilities of setting up an adventure travel company, Jonny Bealby met the woman of his dreams. Not only that, but Rachel was the person with whom he could live out his dream – to travel the Old Silk Road on horseback. On his return to Pakistan that Christmas, however, Jonny was faced with those dreadful words: 'I've met somebody else . . .'

With his heart fixed on this journey, Jonny set out and found Sarah. Unfortunately, their fledgling friendship was soon beset by problems of communication, inexperience and the difficulty of adapting to radically different cultures and surroundings.

'An absolute page-turner . . .' *Wanderlust*

arrow books

Buy *Arrow*

Order further *Arrow* titles from your local bookshop, or have them
delivered directly to your door by Bookpost

The Luck Factor	0099443244	£6.99
The Many Faces of Men	009946635X	£6.99
True Brits	0099453460	£6.99
Your Back, Your Health	0099468026	£9.99
I Didn't Get Where I Am Today	009942164X	£7.99
A Stupid Boy	009944142X	£7.99
Confessions of Reformed Dieter	0099471493	£6.99
The Gangs of New York	0099436744	£7.99
The Gangs of San Francisco	0099455129	£7.99
The Gangs of New Orleans	0099455080	£7.99
Running with the Moon	0099436655	£7.99
For a Pagan Song	0099436736	£7.99
Silk Dreams, Troubled Road	0099414694	£7.99

FREE POST AND PACKING
Overseas customers allow £2 per paperback

PHONE: 01624 677237

POST: Random House Books
c/o Bookpost, PO Box 29, Douglas
Isle of Man, IM99 1BQ

FAX: 01624 670923

EMAIL: bookshop@enterprise.net

Cheques (payable to Bookpost) and credit cards accepted

Prices and availability subject to change without notice
Allow 28 days for delivery
*When placing your order, please state if you do not wish to receive
any additional information*

www.randomhouse.co.uk